Le

THE UNIVERSITY OF WINCHESTER

Martial Rose Library
Tel: 01962 827306

To be returned on or before the day marked above, subject to recall.

Marquette Studies in Philosophy
Andrew Tallon, editor

Lenin As Philosopher
A Critical Examination of the Philosophical Basis of Leninism

Anton Pannekoek

Revised Edition
Edited, annotated, and with an Introduction by Lance Byron Richey

Marquette University Press   2003

MARQUETTE
UNIVERSITY

PRESS

Marquette Studies in Philosophy No. 31
Series Editor, Andrew Tallon

Library of Congress Cataloging-in-Publication Data

Pannekoek, Anton, 1873-1960.
[Lenin als Philosoph. English]
Lenin as philosopher : a critical examination of the philosophical
basis of Leninism / by Anton Pannekoek ; edited, annotated, and with an
introduction by Lance Byron Richey.— Rev. ed.
   p. cm. — (Marquette studies in philosophy ; no. 31)
Includes bibliographical references and index.
ISBN 0-87462-654-4 (pbk. : alk. paper)
1. Lenin, Vladimir Ilyich, 1870-1924. I. Richey, Lance Byron, 1966-
II. Title. III. Marquette studies in philosophy ; #31.
B4249.L384P2713 2003
335.43'092—dc21
                                                        2003007415

Series Editor's Note. Brief history of the text. Original German edition, entitled
*Lenin als Philosoph: Kritische Betrachtung der philosophischen Grundlagen des
Leninismus,* published in Amsterdam, Holland, in 1938, under the pseudonym
John Harper by the Bibliothek der "Ratekorrespondenz" No. 1. Ausgabe der Gruppe
Internationaler Kommunisten. French translation 1947 in *Internationalisme* the
journal of the Gauche Communiste de France. English translation by the author,
Pannekoek, published in in New York by New Essays Press in 1948. See the editor's
Note on the Text, page 62 (infra) for more details on the text. This is the first
scholarly edition in English; the editor corrected the English (Pannekoek was not
fluent in English) using the posthumous 1969 German edition and made other
editorial emendations.

Member, American Association of University Presses

MARQUETTE UNIVERSITY PRESS
MILWAUKEE

The Association of Jesuit University Presses

Contents

Series Editor's Note
Pannekoek had 3 notes, on p. 136 (note A), p. 139 (note B), and p. 151 (note C); these notes appear on page 163. All other notes are the Editor's (Richey).

Pannekoek, Lenin, and the Future of Marxist Philosophy

Anton Pannekoek's *Lenin as Philosopher* occupies a unique position within the literature on Lenin. Some eighty years after Lenin's death and nearly a century after the appearance of his *Materialism and Empirio–criticism*, Pannekoek's slim volume remains one of the most substantive and focused discussions of Lenin's materialist philosophy available.[1] Moreover, it is unsurpassed (at least within the English literature) for its detailed discussion of the late–nineteenth century background to Lenin's thought, a period in the history of philosophy largely forgotten today even by most scholars. For that reason alone, Pannekoek's book merits reading and reflection, and not just by students of the history of Marxism but by anyone interested in the course of modern intellectual history.

Moreover, with the exception of Georg Lukacs, whose small book on Lenin—really just a longish essay—is curiously unphilosophical (or at least unmetaphysical), *Lenin as Philosopher* is the only serious assessment of Lenin's thought written by a major figure in revolutionary politics.[2] As a result, few other works offer such a creative connection of his philosophy (of 1908, at least) to his subsequent political activity—perhaps the most important question of all when assessing his philosophy from a Marxist perspective.[3] If, as Lenin himself demanded, Marxist theory is to be done not by scholars but by revolutionaries, this is no small consideration in assessing its ultimate value. The judgment of Karl Korsch—certainly a comparable figure within Marxist politics and an even larger one within Marxist theory—that Pannekoek, because of his unique combination of scientific training and political activism, "undoubtedly . . . is better qualified for this task than any other contemporary Marxist," still holds true.[4]

Most importantly, reading *Lenin as Philosopher* at the beginning of the twenty–first century offers a new opportunity to reconsider the history of Marxist philosophy—or, more accurately, the philosophy of a once–dominant but now widely discredited strain of Marxism. This is not to say that Pannekoek's final judgments on Lenin should be allowed to stand unchallenged, but rather that he offers an excellent place from which to begin rethinking the significance of Lenin's thought for the Marxist tradition. Indeed, only by considering the unique historical juncture between philosophy, science, and politics which produced both *Materialism and Empirio–criticism* in 1908 and *Lenin as Philosopher* some thirty years later, can Lenin's originality—and Pannekoek's limitations—as a philosopher be fully appreciated.

Towards that goal, this essay is divided into two main sections: (1) a review and interpretation of the philosophical background to Lenin's *Materialism and Empirio–criticism*, supplementing and reinterpreting the account found in Pannekoek's book, and (2) a analysis of the philosophical efforts of Pannekoek and Lenin to escape the impasse of late nineteenth century bourgeois philosophy and of the reasons for Lenin's success and Pannekoek's failure in this project. While the first section makes no pretense to great originality or insight, in the second I do hope to suggest—a suggestion only, given the limitations of this introduction—that *Materialism and Empirio–criticism* has a significance for Marxist philosophy that has yet to be fully appreciated. As will become clear, I believe that this work, despite its many weaknesses, played an essential role in Lenin's larger project of overcoming the self–contradictions of nineteenth century bourgeois philosophy. As such, it deserves much more serious consideration and analysis than either Pannekoek or many of Lenin's own disciples have given it since its appearance.

The Philosophical Background of Materialism and Empirio–criticism

While most students of the history of Marxism know at least the main thrust of Lenin's *Materialism and Empirio–criticism*, and could perhaps even describe in broad outline the philosophical views of Ernst Mach which precipitated a small crisis within Marxism during the first decade of the twentieth century, their knowledge usually ends there. The philosophical milieu out of which the "Machist" controversy arose, namely, the decay of positivism into competing materialist and idealist systems during the last decades of the nineteenth century, has almost entirely disappeared from the historical consciousness of all but a few specialists. This gap in the popular memory is particularly distressing when we recall that positivism and its by–products dominated European philosophy during both the most productive years of Marx's career and the critical period between the appearance of the first volume of *Capital* in 1867 and the appearance of *Materialism and Empirio–criticism* in 1908. Unless one agrees with his Soviet hagiographers that Leninism sprang from Marx's corpus, like Minerva from Zeus' head, fully grown and intellectually mature, this historical amnesia presents an almost insuperable obstacle to the proper understanding of Lenin's ideas.

One of the chief merits of *Lenin as Philosopher* is its ability to help one to gain some familiarity with such now–forgotten figures as Dietzgen, Haeckel, Avenarius, and Mach. At least as regards the particulars of their thought, Pannekoek's book remains one of the quickest and most painless paths to a basic understanding of their positions. This fact alone covers a multitude of intellectual sins, since only one who has suffered through the original texts of these men can fully appreciate the service which Pannekoek's summary provides to modern readers. Less satisfactory, though, is his understanding of the period *in toto*, including his assessments of relative importance of these philosophers and the crude dialectic which governs his historical narrative. Despite his considerable scientific accomplishments, Pannekoek possesses neither nuance or sophistication as an intellectual historian. As a result, his portrait of the philosophical background of

Materialism and Empirio–criticism, which he *de facto* divides into three main schools (Materialism, Idealism, and Marxism), requires both supplementation and occasional correction.

Towards that end, the following discussion—actually only a sketch—of the course of late nineteenth century German philosophy is offered. No pretense of exhaustiveness or even a special thoroughness is made: following the narratives of both Pannekoek and Lenin, such influential figures of the period such as Weber, Frege, and Nietzsche are noticeably absent. Even the discussion of the more prominent figures in *Lenin as Philosopher*, such as Dietzgen and Haeckel, is limited to the provision of a short summary of their positions, especially when Pannekoek has failed to provide this. Rather, the primary purpose of this section is to recast the historical narrative offered by Pannekoek, to emphasize the common origins, assumptions, and limitations of these thinkers, and to present the conflict between materialism and idealism as the expression of a more fundamental philosophical kinship among philosophers of the period. Only when they are understood thus can the Lenin's originality and importance as a philosopher be clearly seen.

(A) Positivism

Perhaps the most serious weakness of Pannekoek's reconstruction of the period is his failure to note the common source of both "middle-class" materialism and Machism in the decay of positivism from the 1850s onwards. While almost every textbook history of the period locates the source of both materialism and Machism in positivism, and many even extend the name "positivist" to include them all, Pannekoek treats them as philosophically (if not socially) discrete movements. Moreover, his portrait of them is both ideologically charged and crudely schematic, with materialism embodying the initial stage of bourgeois triumph over feudalism, and idealism consisting of little more than a reactionary response to the rising power of the proletariat. Whatever polemical purposes such a presentation of their relations may serve, it does little to further the reader's understanding of the background to Lenin's thought. Worse still, by not locating the origin of both movements in the positivism of the mid–

nineteenth century, Pannekoek failed to see how Lenin's work transcends their common problematic and thereby makes an original and valuable contribution to Marxist philosophy. This omission by Pannekoek is all the more curious when one considers the importance of positivism for understanding the era. Leaving aside its founder Auguste Comte's much–maligned attempt late in life to convert it into a secular version of Catholicism, what Ted Benton has called positivism's "intellectual–cum–political project" was in fact one of the first serious attempts to apply the methodology of the natural sciences to the study and reform of modern society.[5] As such, positivism embodied the self–image of the bourgeoisie, conceiving itself as a truly scientific (as opposed to metaphysical or idealistic) philosophy supporting a progressive but non–revolutionary political program.

Modeling itself on the practical assumptions of contemporary science, positivism espoused a reductivist materialism for its ontology while committing itself to an empiricist epistemology according to which human consciousness was capable of knowing all aspects of the world without exception.[6] Science displaced philosophy both theoretically and practically, with all primary research into the nature of the world belonging to the former and philosophy's task limited to the correlating and systematizing the findings of otherwise autonomous scientific disciplines. By dispensing with traditional metaphysics, positivism hoped to overcome the ontological dualism of early modern philosophy while at the same time avoiding the agnosticism of Hume and Kant. Unfortunately, the underlying conflict between an materialist ontology which rejected any special status for consciousness and an empiricist epistemology which limited all knowledge of the physical world to what could be known or inferred from sense data, a conflict which had troubled all of eighteenth century philosophy, was rarely even recognized by the early positivists, much less resolved by them.

If the philosophical project of positivism relied too much on the practical activity of science and too little on speculative efforts to undergird it, it political and social project was equally uncritical. Extending these anti–metaphysical attitudes beyond the physical realm to the social sciences, positivism at the same time proposed the gradual and systematic application of the methods of empirical science for resolving the problems of contemporary society, with social engineers taking the place of social theorists and political activists. This insistence that social change be initiated and administered by a technically educated elite rather than by mass political action (which led Marx to dismiss Comte as a peddler of *Scheisspositivismus*—"shit positivism") clearly identifies positivism as a fundamentally bourgeois and conservative movement. Certainly, both the supreme confidence it placed in both the objectivity of modern science and in the rational perfectibility of the social order through social engineering was accepted without question by the bourgeoisie of the era.

Of course, any short summary runs the risk of overstating the unity and coherence of positivism, which frequently operated outside of narrow academic circles more as a scientific (or, more accurately, scientistic) *weltanschauung* than as a tightly structured philosophical system. And, in truth, the popularity of positivism owed as much—if not more—to political and economic developments within European society as to any intrinsic philosophical merit it may have possessed. In short, positivism promised a scientific alternative to both the intellectual and social problems of the modern age in an era when the philosophical and political movements of the first half of the century appeared to have exhausted and discredited themselves. As such, it was initially received with great enthusiasm and quickly spread across most of the continent, in the process adapting itself to local intellectual and political concerns to a remarkable degree.[7]

In the German speaking regions of Central Europe, where Pannekoek and Lenin focused their attention, the political goals of positivism received much less notice that its philosophical foundations and it was widely considered a successor to the idealist and post–idealist systems dominant in the earlier part of the century. This exaggerated confidence in its philosophical sophistication, though, was unfounded, as positivism proved ill–prepared for the sort of rigorous analysis it received—apparently for the first time—there. Almost immediately, the unresolved tension between its two main philosophical pillars, materialism and empiricism, which had been suppressed during its earliest period by the humanism and utopian socialism of Comte and Saint–Simon, reappeared. After the failed revolutions of 1848, and with the forces of reaction and nationalism triumphant in Germany and elsewhere, the political hopes of an earlier positivism could no longer disguise the theoretical conflicts within it. As a result, these opposing tendencies split apart by the 1850s, forming two relatively well–defined (and predominantly but not exclusively German) camps that would do battle for the remainder of the century.

(B) Materialism

The first movement to clearly emerge from the decay of positivism was materialism (Pannekoek adds the sobriquet "middle–class"), which was really little more than a renovated version of the eighteenth century French materialism found in Lamettrie, Diderot and others, but stripped of what little epistemological sophistication positivism had since been added to it. While forgotten now, figures such as Moleschott, Vogt, Büchner, and Haeckel were leaders in the resurgence of mechanistic materialism as an influential philosophical movement in the middle of the century.[8] Unlike the giants of earlier generations such as Hegel and Feuerbach, these thinkers had backgrounds not in history and philosophy but rather in the biological sciences, especially medicine. The emphasis on the physical rather than the rational characteristics of the human person such training required naturally led them in different philosophical directions than their idealist predecessors. However, they ultimately proved so eager to provide a philosophical framework for the materialistic assumptions of modern science that they almost completely overlooked the epistemological problems raised by its empirical methods.

The pioneer of this new movement was Jacob Moleschott, a physician whose research into the nervous system and the role of chemical activity in brain activity led him to attempt a purely materialist (and rather unsophisticated) account of human consciousness and emotions. In particular, Moleschott attempted to draw connections between the presence of trace elements in the human diet and the performance of various physical activities (e.g., his keen interest in the role of phosphorus in proper mental activity). While considerably less successful as a philosopher than as a scientist (his main claim to philosophical fame is that his work inspired Feuerbach's dictum "Man is what he eats"), with his magnum opus *Der Krieslauf des Lebens* (*The Cycle of Life*) Moleschott helped lay the foundations for modern biochemistry by his research into the chemical and material bases of living organisms.[9] Moreover, his scientific sophistication (in comparison to eighteenth century materialists) made Moleschott's reductivist materialism seem revolutionary to many contemporaries.

Foremost among these was Karl Vogt, a geologist turned zoologist, who built upon Moleschott's work in order to explicitly deny the existence of the human soul—at the time an act of both philosophical and social radicalism. Arguing for a reductivist account of consciousness, Vogt employed his famous (and quite unfortunate) analogy between the liver's secretion of bile and the brain's production of thought.[10] While this glossing over of the philosophical problem of consciousness may have had a certain currency because of its pithiness, it certainly did not mark any appreciable advance in the attempt to conceptualize consciousness within a materialist framework. Not surprisingly, Vogt is best remembered as the target of Marx's vitriol in *Herr Vogt* and not for any lasting contributions to the materialist theory of mind.

The writings of the physiologist Ludwig Büchner, which were enormously popular among educated readers in Germany throughout the 1850s and 1860s, reveal a similar contrast between scientific sophistication and philosophical naivete.[11] While Moleschott and Vogt had generally limited their materialism to anthropological concerns, Büchner attempted a more comprehensive version of materialism. In *Kraft and Stoff*, he sought to explain all phenomena solely in terms of matter endowed with force (hence the title of his book), denied any immaterial reality in nature, and considered the soul to be merely a comprehensive concept for the physical functioning of the organism in response to its environment. Rejecting any belief in teleology within the natural order, Büchner considered consciousness, character, and culture nothing more than specific and determined results of necessary natural processes. At the same time, though, he refused to give a systematic account of the metaphysical principles underlying his materialism. As regards the relationship between consciousness and its material substratum, he was particularly vague. At times he sim-

ply identified matter and consciousness, tending towards a materialistic monism, while later he suggested that matter and mind may
both be reducible to some more fundamental but unknown reality
(echoing here Comte's quasi–mystical reverence for the "unknown"
foundation of the world which appeared in his last writings). In any
case, Büchner's materialism never went beyond the philosophical limitations of Moleschott and Vogt's work.

This brand of biological materialism found its fullest and final expression in the writings of Ernest Haeckel. Trained as a physician,
Haeckel abandoned medicine after reading *The Origin of Species* in
1859 and devoted the remainder of his life (a full sixty years, until his
death in 1919) to comparative anatomy and biology, making contributions of importance in both fields.[12] However, his most influential
writings were not in science but in popular philosophy, beginning in
the 1870s and culminating in his *The Riddle of the World* in 1899
(which is still in print over a century later). There Haeckel offered
the fullest exposition of his philosophy, in which an eclectic combination of materialism and evolutionary theory was employed to explain not only the appearance and development of the physical and
biological orders in nature but also the differentiation of humanity
into assorted races, classes, and nations.[13]

Despite his lack of any formal training in philosophy, Haeckel
showed a greater awareness of the problems involved in vulgar materialism than his predecessors did and actively tried to meet them. To
avoid the criticism which greeted the materialism of Moleschott, Vogt,
and Büchner, Haeckel classified himself as a "monist" rather than a
materialist per se, believing all matter to be infused with some sort of
consciousness or energy. As was the case with Büchner, though, the
philosophical problems which this position raised about the ontological status of consciousness (e.g., whether inorganic compounds
also count as conscious beings insofar as they exist) and the epistemic
status of knowledge (e.g., beliefs are either true or false, but it is
unclear whether it makes sense to describe states of matter thus) were
never adequately addressed, much less resolved, by him.[14] And, while
Haeckel never completely or even coherently defended his version of
pan–psychism, the fact that he professed it rather than the vulgar
materialism of Vogt or Moleschott shows at least an intuitive aware-

ness by him of the philosophical problems involved in materialism (an awareness largely lacking in his predecessors). But Haeckel never came to an adequate understanding, much less resolution, of the issues involved. Ultimately, Haeckel's monism was as much a philosophical dead end as that of Büchner, and even one of his most sympathetic critics concedes "the main criticism which the idealists of Germany made against Haeckel, ... [namely, either] that he did not have an adequate theory of knowledge, or that it was not even present."[15]

The problem which had confronted earlier materialists, namely, the privileged epistemic status of science within an ontologically undifferentiated natural order, remained unanswered. Indeed, in some respects Haeckel's insistence on monism rather than materialism is simply an acknowledgment of the inability of the materialist impulse in German post–positivism to resolve the philosophical tensions which had previously doomed positivism. The fundamental problem common to all the materialisms discussed—namely, their inability within a mechanistic materialism to provide a secure epistemic foundation for science—is never even explicitly acknowledged by him. Thus, Haeckel's failure is not only a personal one, but in effect completes the failure of this entire school of materialism.

(C) Idealism

If a purely materialist solution to the contradictions of positivism both culminated and collapsed in the writings of Haeckel, it is in the writings of Ernst Mach and Richard Avenarius that we find the empiricist elements of positivism played out to their logical conclusion. The fact that Pannekoek felt obliged to discuss their views at such length and with such atypical even–handedness is a testimony both to their prestige among contemporary philosophers and to the power and promise of their philosophical project. However, their attempt to give methodological priority to positivism's epistemology over its ontology, while considerably more philosophically astute, was ultimately no more successful than earlier materialist theories at resolving the philosophical tensions within positivism.

When discussing Mach's philosophy and his distance from the materialism of the period, it must be noted that his original training was as a physicist rather than a physician or biologist. Because Mach seems to have felt with a particular intensity the tension between the indirect and inductive methods of modern physics and the ideal of logical certainty in the descriptions and predictions of natural phenomena which it promised, he paid much greater attention to questions of scientific methodology and epistemology than any of the materialists of his era. Even when he developed an interest in psychology and the physiology of sensation in the 1860s and 1870s, fields then dominated by materialistically inclined physiologists and neurologists, his primary concern was not with their biological foundations but rather in their epistemic implications for science.

Mach's intellectual development was also assisted by the fact that he was well read in philosophy—especially Hume and Berkeley, whose appeals to sense data and common sense over metaphysical speculation greatly influenced his thought. Refusing to follow materialism in its simple identification of mental events with the functions of the brain, Mach instead attempted to reduce all scientific and practical concepts (including those of time, space, and the knowing subject) and all objects of experience to a pure and pre–metaphysical field of sense data. Like Hume, he considered all physical objects (including his own body) and the conceptual categories used to think them to be methodologically posterior to and constructed out of the immediately given data of sense experience—at least as regards their epistemic status as possible objects of knowledge. At the same time, he rejected as metaphysical and unscientific all forms of Kantian apriorism whereby some features of the world are not grounded in experience but rather in the cognitive structures of the knowing subject.

In this regard, Mach was especially faithful to the scientific and "positive" ideals of positivism, and believed himself to be conducting a truly scientific investigation both of the structure of knowledge and of the world. Like the Logical Positivists of the twentieth century who followed him, Mach dreamed of limiting himself to the realm of pure experience and was reluctant to make metaphysical claims about the nature of the world which would not have an immediate cash–value for scientific investigation. Thus, for example, he considered the physical/psychical distinction which had so troubled materialism not an ultimate ontological difference in the external world but rather simply a methodological and explanatory one within science, to be accepted for pragmatic reasons as the most economical way to organize experience into a useful and consistent system. Whatever the weaknesses of this attempted solution, it is a marked improvement over the outdated materialism outlined above.

Ultimately, though, Mach's attempt to fit the empiricist aspects of positivism to the more sophisticated scientific demands of the late nineteenth century proved equally unsatisfactory. Far from building upon Kant's transcendental idealism, Mach's idealism resulted in a regression to the pre–critical problems of Hume and Berkeley which Kant believed himself to have overcome. Indeed, all the problems of the unity and agency of the knowing subject which had bedeviled Hume returned with a vengeance in Mach's philosophy. Absent a transcendental subject or an underlying biological system to support it, it is never clear in Mach's writings what the source of the organizing principle which economically arranges sense data into a coherent realm is, and he never satisfactorily accounted for the unity of the knowing subject which was one of the express goals of Kant's transcendental idealism.

Furthermore, as was also with the case with Berkeley and Hume, the methodological priority which Mach gives to sense data constantly threatens to slip into an ontological priority, resulting in a version of subjective idealism in which the objects of knowledge have no existence apart from the knowing subject. Of course, Mach denied the charge of idealism, and generally considered the existence of an external world as the only possible assumption a working scientist can make. However, he is hardly consistent in applying this realist assumption to his philosophical account of knowledge. In his *Principles of the Theory of Heat*, Mach went so far as to deny the existence of atoms and molecules because, however useful they may be to the construction of a coherent science of nature, they are not capable of being perceived but are instead only inferred from a larger theoretical framework about the construction of matter.[16] As a result of his ambiguity about the status of the external world, Mach was interpreted idealistically even among his most sympathetic supporters, the most important of whom was Richard Avenarius.

Unlike Mach or any of the materialists discussed, Avenarius was a trained philosopher and taught at Zurich throughout his professional career. While certainly an epigone of Mach, Avenarius did bring to his work a greater systematicity and technicality which, at the very least, revealed the inherent limitations of his radical empiricism. The most important amendment made by Avenarius to Mach's system was his attempt to overcome the problem of the subject (a persistent one for both Hume and Mach) with the "principle of coordination." According to Avenarius, the traditional division of the world into subject and object is due to "introjection," that is, the erroneous inference to a true world underlying and concealed by the appearances which constitute the object of human knowledge. Both the skepticism of Hume and the transcendental idealism of Kant, Avenarius suggested, arose from an underlying assumption that an unknowable world existed beyond and behind our subjective sense impressions. By rejecting the belief that the self or subject is irreducible to experience and is forever separated from the world by its ideas, Avenarius believed that the skepticism and subjectivism of earlier philosophical systems could be avoided since there is no longer any absolute opposition between "my" experience of the world and the world itself. In short, introjection creates the problem of subjectivism by positing the concept of a subject separate from the objective world. Instead, Avenarius insisted with Mach that there is only "pure" experience out of which both subjects and objects are constructed.

At the same time, the fact that a unitary world is known from a variety of perspectives (and, therefore, seemingly by multiple subjects) demands explanation. To do this, Avenarius introduces the "principle of coordination." Using it, an otherwise undifferentiated field of pure consciousness (which is not populated by either metaphysical or transcendental subjects, as with Descartes and Kant) can be described from multiple perspectives by the employment of "coordinating principles" whereby any given point within this field interrelates all other points in reference to itself. Hence, "my" knowledge of the world is in fact the coordination of the field of consciousness described as if there were a central principle uniting and gathering them into a single and self–consistent realm of experience, while "your" experience is simply the same field of experience ordered around a different coordinating principle.

Ultimately, though, Avenarius' attempt to get around the problem of the subject by replacing introjection with the principle of coordination fails. Exactly what it is that effects this coordination which "I" experience remains obscure. Although in fact there is no entity (either substantial or transcendental) effecting such a coordination, the concept of the self remains a necessary component of any description of experience since there is no "view from nowhere" around which experience could be objectively and absolutely ordered. Avenarius rejects a transcendental subject on principle, while any materialist or biological reductionism would run into his decision to privilege pure sense experience—a manifest contradiction. Leszek Kolakowski presents the problem thus:

> It is in fact hard to reconcile the two fundamental categories of 'introjection' and 'principle [of] co–ordination.' The critique of introjection is intended to do away with the 'subject' as a superfluous construction and with the distinction between 'subjective' and 'objective' Being. Experience is left as an ontologically neutral zone, whose relation to 'being–in–itself' cannot be meaningfully inquired into. Epistemological aspirations are relinquished, and science is left to deal with its problems as they are, without ontological interpretation. This is how Mach understood the matter. If, however, we also adopt the theory of 'principle [of] coordination', the subject, under a different name, reappears as a separate category, whose inevitable presence in experience can only be understood on the assumption that it is the knower and not the known—yet Avenarius rejects this supposition. If we accept both parts of his interpretation [of Mach], the result may easily lead us into an absurdity: the self, as a component of experience on the same footing as things, is for some unintelligible reason the condition of the appearance of all its other components. The inadmissability of this is clear when Avenarius identifies the 'central term' of co–ordination with the human nervous system— so that the latter, a physical object, is the condition of the presence of all other physical objects. Avenarius does not, of course, state this

absurd conclusion, but it is hard to see how it can be avoided if both his basic tenets are maintained.[17]

The most important point to note here is not that Mach and Avenarius had idealist tendencies: indeed, as Kolakowski shows, Avenarius was more than willing to appeal to a biological or material source of knowledge to avoid his problems. Rather, the real philosophical failure is their inability to make positivism self–consistent by following its epistemological assumptions to their limit. With his failure to resolve the problem of the subject, Avenarius marks (as did Haeckel for the materialists) the failure of idealism to break out of the philosophical impasse within positivism. Even after some fifty years of work, in the first decade of the twentieth century the deadlock between materialist ontology and empiricist epistemology, which constituted the central failure of nineteenth century bourgeois philosophy, remained unbroken.

(D) Marxism

Despite Engels' claims to the contrary, Marx's work did not form a complete and systematic theory of reality in the way which, for instance, Hegel's did (or attempted to do). Rather, Marx bequeathed to European socialism a general theory of social development built upon an only partially developed and never satisfactorily elaborated philosophical foundation. While unmistakably materialist and dialectical in character, Marx's underlying metaphysical assumptions were capable of development in a variety of directions. With the rapid advance of science and socialist politics during the last decades of the nineteenth century, such development and elaboration proved not only intellectually irresistible but practically unavoidable. Thus, it is not surprising that both the vulgar materialism and the idealism of the period competed as possible philosophical idioms in which to recast Marx. These attempts to update Marxism, in turn, were the primary medium through which both Pannekoek and Lenin received and interpreted their bourgeois philosophical heritage. Hence, a clearer understanding of them is necessary to appreciate the originality of Lenin's thought.

(i) Dietzgen

Ironically, the vulgar materialism of the period made its greatest in-roads into Marxism through the efforts of the man who coined the term "dialectical materialism," Joseph Dietzgen. His terminological accomplishment notwithstanding, the space devoted by Pannekoek in *Lenin as Philosopher* to the thought of Joseph Dietzgen is, by any meaningful philosophical standard, clearly excessive. In general, Dietzgen's level of philosophical sophistication did not rise above that of his non–dialectical materialist counterparts, Haeckel and Büchner (with whose work his writings had many similarities), and fell con-siderably short of that of either Mach or Avenarius. Despite their occasional and not unambiguous praise for him, Dietzgen the phi-losopher was indulged by Marx and Engels much more for the sake of his political activities in the First International than for any origi-nal intellectual content his writings contained.[18] Indeed, his funda-mental confusion on central philosophical topics could not be hid-den even from so sympathetic a reader as Lenin, who writes that "Dietzgen sinned much by his clumsy deviations from [Marx and Engels' dialectical understanding of] materialism."[19]

Chief among these errors was an understanding of "dialectical materialism" which was considerably more materialist than dialecti-cal—in fact, which was not dialectical at all but essentially positivist in character. For Dietzgen, "dialectical thinking" was the ability of the mind to unify different qualities and aspects of the natural order within a single object of thought, without admitting the existence of more fundamental oppositions and contradictions within the world. John Gerber writes:

> This abstraction process [of the human mind] is dialectical in the sense that it mediates differences and distinctions in a particular object of thought. For Dietzgen, however, dialectical did not always mean absolute opposites or contradictions. These distinc-tions existed only through the mental separation of the component parts of a particular object of thought. *Without the mental act there could be no contradictions* [emphasis added]. The mind merely constructs them and makes them relative and equal as part of the classification and systematization process.[20]

Dietzgen in effect reduced the dialectic of nature to a cognitive process of the human mind in its attempt to organize and systematize the contents drawn from of sense experience (Dietzgen's empiricism is manifest throughout his writings), a project drawn directly from positivism rather than Hegel or Marx.

On one level, this is neither surprising nor especially troubling. As Gerber notes, "Considered in overall terms, Dietzgen was essentially a philosopher of science, attempting to develop the methodology for a comprehensive view of the world for the purposes of prediction and control, a fact which doubtless made a marked impression on the young Pannekoek."[21] As such, Dietzgen quite naturally adopted the positivism of the era, making only the minimal criticisms and adjustments required by his acceptance of a Marxist political program. In keeping with the general thrust of scientific positivism, he believed that the mind, through its faculties of inference and induction, is able to create and develop (in a somewhat unspecified but nominally "dialectical" manner) systems of concepts and categories which will ever more fully and rationally approximate the infinite variety and essential unity of the natural order. The inexhaustibility of nature is mirrored in the infinite capacity of the human mind for intellectual development and the creation of ever more sophisticated and adequate conceptual schemes. Science is thereby defended in principle and forever open to criticism and correction in practice, especially in light of Marxist critiques of the bourgeois society which produces its practicioners.

Ultimately, though, as a result of his vitiation of dialectics and substitution for it of a positivist theory of knowledge, Dietzgen's Marxism by necessity became a much more "regional" science, functioning not as a governing framework for all explanations but rather as a social theory capable of being inserted into a larger and more traditional philosophy of science. As Gerber notes, "Although his dialectics rejected any rigid laws of a universal system, Dietzgen accepted (at least in a relative sense) Marx's social theories that explain social change and class ideologies in terms of the fundamental relations of economic production."[22] However, by attempting "to clarify these theories by making explicit their psychological assumptions through an inductive theory of cognition," he believed he could ground this

social theory in a larger, non–dialectical theory of nature more ame-
nable to investigation by traditional scientific methods:

> Dietzgen, by making the human mind the special subject of
> investigation, and by attempting to show the exact content of the
> process of human consciousness, has [in Pannekoek's opinion]
> made a major contribution to filling this gap [between conscious-
> ness and matter in bourgeois philosophy]. Because it validated
> empirical methodology itself, Dietzgen's scientific and experi-
> ence–based theory of human thinking constituted the "essence and
> foundation" of Marx's theory of society and man.[23]

Having thus removed the dialectic from nature and made it instead a cognitive process, Dietzgen's materialism was by definition
non–dialectical, his nomenclature notwithstanding. Not surprisingly,
it was also almost completely unoriginal. In fact, one finds in
Dietzgen's writings about materialism not an advance beyond or even
a restatement of Marx's views but instead a largely uncritical repetition of the views of Moleschott, Vogt and Büchner (Haeckel's "monism" appeared after the period in which Dietzgen wrote). Their rejection of any form of dualism in a favor of a mechanistic and materialistic account of nature is accepted without question or development. Noticeably absent from his writings is any serious attempt to
resolve or even recognize the serious problems associated with their
views (unless one believes that pairing the adjective "dialectical" with
the noun "materialism" constitutes a philosophical breakthrough).

This failure was not lost on most Marxists of his and subsequent
eras. Despite enjoying a certain popularity and readership in the closing decades of the nineteenth century, due no doubt to Marx's polite
praise, Dietzgen's prestige went into serious decline at the beginning
of the twentieth century and since 1908 his popularity has declined
precipitously and, in all likelihood, permanently. Although Dietzgen
temporarily retained some popularity within small circles, especially
among some Dutch Marxists such as Pannekoek, the simultaneous
rise of both a systematic Soviet Marxism and Western Marxism in
the 1920s quickly revealed his serious philosophical limitations and
effectively ended his influence. Even Pannekoek's extensive discussion and defense of him in *Lenin as Philosopher* in 1938 only repli-

cates without significant addition his introduction to a collection of Dietzgen's writings issued some thirty years earlier.[24] The ultimate insignificance of Dietzgen for subsequent Marxist philosophy is shown by the fact Leszek Kolakowski's monumental history of Marxism passes him over in complete silence.[25]

Ultimately, Dietzgen's version of dialectical materialism never solves either the ontological or epistemological questions which plagued earlier versions of materialism (a fact which Pannekoek's idolization of Dietzgen in *Lenin as Philosopher* cannot conceal) because, at the most basic level, he attempted to do Marxist philosophy with a set of ontological concepts borrowed wholesale from the bourgeois materialism of the 1850s and 1860s. And if he avoided the greater part of Lenin's wrath in *Materialism and Empirio–criticism*, it was not because of any particular value his thought had for Marxism so much as the irrelevance it had for most educated thinkers whose own philosophical theories posed a greater and more immediate danger for Marxist theory and practice.

(ii) Machism

Among these more dangerous philosophies was the idealism of Mach which, beginning in the 1890s and climaxing in the first decade of the twentieth century, made serious in–roads into Marxist philosophy, especially within Russia, and for a brief period promised a way out of the quite unsatisfying appropriations of Marx by such materialists as Dietzgen. Because of its role as the catalyst for Lenin's *Materialism and Empirio–criticism*, the development and details of the Machist controversy, both as a political and a philosophical struggle within Russian Marxism, has received considerable attention over the last several decades. Robert C. Williams has detailed the political aspects of the Machist controversy and the manner in which philosophical ideas served as a mask for intra–party conflicts to an extent normally not appreciated by students of Leninism.[26] However, to reduce the Machist controversy to a purely or even primarily political battle (as Williams tends to do) is to overlook the key philosophical questions which it raised and which Lenin clearly believed were of central importance not only to Marxist philosophy but to Marxist revolutionary theory as well. And, while no exhaustive discussion is possible here, a basic introduction to the central themes of Russian Machism is essential for appreciating both the weaknesses of Pannekoek's Marxism and the strength of Lenin's.

As Kolakowski points out, in many ways the rise of Machism reflects a generational crisis within Marxism, as the rationality and scientific optimism typical of the period of the First International (and typified by Dietzgen) was supplanted by a new generation of thinkers who reflected the growing unease and pessimism within the Western intellectual scene from the 1890s onward. Part of the reason for the loss of faith in science and reason which many Marxists felt was the crisis in modern physics, to which Mach's philosophy was but one (albeit very important) response. This scientific crisis (see the below, pp. 51–52), though, was only one aspect of a much broader cultural shift epitomized by the increased popularity of such writers as Nietzsche and Dostoyevsky and finding its expression throughout the whole of the artistic and intellectual community, where "pessimism, Satanism, apocalyptic prophecies, the search for the mystic and metaphysical depths, love of the fantastic, eroticism, psychology and self–analysis—all these merged into a single modernistic culture."[27] It is not surprising that a man such as Lenin would have any more sympathy for these morbidly narcissistic pursuits, which he (correctly) saw to be serving the emotional needs of a decadent intelligentsia at the expense of focused and disciplined revolutionary political action, than he did for the idealism of Mach.

Within Russian Marxism, this new intellectual climate manifested itself in the adoption of Machist epistemology by a large segment of the party's intelligentsia. Machism appealed to both Bolshevik and Menshivik theorists and ultimately included such diverse thinkers as Anatoly Lunacharsky, Victor Chernov, and Nikolai Valentinov. Foremost among all these, though, both politically and philosophically, was the Bolshevik Alexander Bogdanov, whose massive *Empiriomonism* constitutes the most ambitious and successful attempt to restate the Marxist political project within the broadly idealist philosophical categories of Avenarius and Mach.[28] Lenin himself viewed Bogdanov as the most important representative of Machism, directing much of his ire and fire against him, and his work can fairly serve as an accurate representative of the general philosophical and political tendencies of the Machism which provoked Lenin into devoting almost all of 1908 to composing *Materialism and Empirio–criticism.* David Rowley has recently recast the debate over Bogdanov's philosophy, which previously had been dominated by Soviet demonizers of him as an apostate from Marxism–Leninism.[29] Instead, Rowley portrays Bogdanov as responding to the intellectual crisis within Marxism occasioned by the former Marxist and subsequent Christian mystic Nikolai Berdyaev's attempt to provide an absolute moral justification to Marxist revolutionary activity by appealing to Kant's ethical theory. Bogdanov believed that reorienting the justification for revolutionary activity around moral rather than historical reasons ran the risk of introducing ethical paralysis and morbid self–examination into the intellectual leadership of Marxism. At the same time, he feared that any attempt to reject the ethical a priori of Kant would also result in the destruction of the a priori laws of nature whose preservation Kant had so desperately sought. Whether or not such a connection between ethics and science actually exists outside a neo–kantian framework is doubtful, but Bogdanov (along with many philosophers of the era) believed it did and felt compelled to find an alternative epistemology which could guarantee the scientific character of Marxism without subordinating the activities of revolutionary agents to a transcendent moral norm.

In Mach's philosophy Bogdanov believed he had found a metaphysic capable of dispensing with the categorical imperative while at the same time preserving the objective and scientific character of Marxist political theory. Rowley writes:

> Following the empiriocriticism of Ernst Mach, Bogdanov espoused a strict empiricism and denied the possibility of a priori knowledge of any sort at all. He explicitly rejected the notion of absolute truth, cause and effect, and absolute time or space—as well as absolute ethical value. Bogdanov defined reality in terms of experience: The real world is identical with human experience of it.[30]

Attempting to build a marxist structure upon this Machist foundation, though, Bogdanov then substitutes for Mach's individual knower
the collective consciousness of society:

> In *Empiriomonism*, the first major collection of his positivist
> writings, Bogdanov illustrated how this was possible. "The basis of
> 'objectivity' must lie in the sphere of collective experience . . . The
> objective character of the physical world consists in the fact that it
> exists not for me individually but for everyone, and for everyone
> has a definite meaning, exactly, I am convinced, as it does for me."
> In this way the sense of the external world, the knowledge, and the
> values of any particular social group are not mere subjective whims
> of individuals. "Reality" is made up of the shared perceptions of the
> collective consciousness of a society. "The physical world is collec-
> tively organized experience."[31]

In any society, Bogdanov recognized, it is ideology which makes
possible concerted human activity through common social and intellectual structures such as religion, language, law, etc. In keeping
with a broadly Leninist theory of revolutionary activity, Bogdanov
argued that the intellectual avant–garde of the revolutionary movement was responsible for challenging and reshaping the ideology of
capitalist society. Only if this was done would the revolutionary activity of a working class ideologically conditioned to accept and operate within the limitations placed upon it by the capitalist class which
created and continues to dominate the realm of ideology become
possible. Thus, Bogdanov argued, both economism, the quietistic
tendency to abandon the course of society to inhuman economic
laws, and ethical idealism, the retreat from concrete political activity
into mysticism and moral narcissism, are abdications of the responsi-
bility of the intelligentsia to lead and shape the proletarian revolutionary movement.

Whatever the purely philosophical merits or demerits of Bogdanov's
empiriomonism or of empirio–criticism in general, its appearance
within the rank of Russian Marxism was as much a political as a
philosophical event, and Lenin responded to it as such in his *Materialism and Empirio–criticism*. In this work, Neil Harding writes, Lenin
"would once and for all denounce his Bolshevik opponents (espe-

cially Bogdanov) as men who had turned their backs on Marx's militant materialism and gone a–whoring after 'modern' relativist philosophical theories which led them, ineluctably, into fideism and rank religiosity."[32] By studying Lenin's attack upon it, the manner in which philosophical theory and political action (or inaction) intersect within Marxism becomes clearer. Especially in light of Pannekoek's decision to pass over this debate in favor of a purely "philosophical" attack upon Lenin's thought, some discussion of how Lenin understood and responded to Bogdanov's work can make clear why he decided to devote almost the entire year of 1908 to refuting what appeared to many (including, apparently, Pannekoek) as a minor theoretical debate within Russian emigré politics.

That Lenin should have opposed Bogdanov's empirio–criticism is hardly obvious, since Bogdanov seemed to have fitted Marxism to a contemporary and scientific philosophy while at the same time avoiding the bourgeois tendency to privilege moralizing over political action. Ultimately, Lenin's objection to Bogdanov and empirio–criticism is based in a critique of the implications such a radically empiricist and even idealist philosophy must have for political activity. Because of Bogdanov's emphasis on collective consciousness as the source of all reality, for him "ideology was not a superstructure but the very foundation of the social system."[33] Hence, any revolutionary activity must begin with the cultural re–education of the revolutionary elite rather than through the political organization and revolutionary activities of the proletariat. To Lenin, Bogdanov's empirio–criticism threatened to change Marxist theory from a political into a cultural and educational force, not directed at political action but rather at the academic exercise of redefining key ideological concepts not as a preliminary to but as a substitute for mass political action. It was just this tendency among the Young Hegelians to confuse intellectual critique with effective political action which Marx and Engels had attacked in *The German Ideology* some sixty years earlier.

Worse yet, by his denial of an independently existing material world which causes, determines and can explain the contents of human consciousness, Bogdanov threatened to relapse into the pre–Marxist belief that history is determined not by objective scientific and social laws but rather by the actions of individual moral agents. This, for

Lenin, was but one step away from relapsing into an outdated religious world view according to which one supreme moral agent, God, directs and determines the ends of history.[34] The purpose of *Materialism and Empirio–criticism*, which was necessarily both a philosophical and a political purpose, was to expose the connections between these seemingly disparate errors. Harding writes:

> What Lenin clearly set out to accomplish was to associate Bogdanov, in spite of his cogent protests to the contrary, with Lunacharsky's overt lapse into a kind of religious anthropomorphism [and] with all the more 'idealistic' utterances of Mach and Avenarius, or any of their disciples, in order to demonstrate the un–Marxist character of Bogdanov's basic epistemological presuppositions—which had led him and his group into petty–bourgeois political tactics.[35]

Lenin's attack on the counter–revolutionary implications of empirio–criticism is vindicated by the subsequent career of Bogdanov himself. Lenin "might have foreseen the inevitable passage from political revolution to cultural education that Bogdanov was going to follow" when, after his expulsion from the Bolshevik party in 1909, Bogdanov took a considerably more tolerant and incremental attitude towards political revolution.[36] As with Berdyaev before him, Bogdanov's rejection of materialism and his search for a more contemporary (and therefore idealistic) philosophical idiom helped to dissipate his revolutionary energies in cultural and ideological rather than directly political activities. In effect, Lenin equated idealism with Machism, and Machism with voluntarism, fideism, and relativism, and rightly rejected them all as incompatible not only with the scientific character of Marxism but with its political character as well. He writes:

> [I]f truth is *only* an ideological form, then there can be no truth independent of the subject, of humanity, for neither Bogdanov nor we know any other ideology but human ideology. . . . if truth is a form of human experience, there can be no truth independent of humanity; there can be no objective truth.[37]

And, drawing the obvious conclusion about the dangers of empirio–criticism to Marxism, Lenin warns that "behind the epistemological scholasticism of empirio–criticism one must not fail to see the struggle of parties in philosophy, a struggle which in the last analysis reflects the tendencies and ideologies of the antagonistic classes in modern society."[38]

Whatever the political motives or consequences of Lenin's assault on Machism, it can hardly be dismissed as merely an intra–party dispute. If anything, it illustrates the intimate connection which Lenin saw between theory and practice within Marxist politics, as well as the problems confronting any Marxist philosophy at the beginning of the twentieth century. If Dietzgen's writings were a threat (albeit a quite minor one) to Marxist theory because of their intellectual deficiencies, then Mach's (and those of his followers) were much greater threats to revolutionary practice because of their intellectual excesses. Pannekoek's purely "philosophical" critique of Lenin overlooks not only these threats to Marxism, but their connections as well. In any case, for Lenin neither Dietzgen's materialism nor Machist idealism was a suitable vehicle for doing Marxist philosophy, despite their pretensions to orthodoxy or scientific competence. In addition, Lenin saw clearly that any new attempt at a Marxist philosophy which could serve as an adequate basis for political action would have to move beyond the impasse within post–positivist thought which saw idealism and vulgar materialism as the only philosophical options.

Breaking the Impasse: Lenin and Pannekoek as Philosophers

In writing *Materialism and Empirio–criticism*, Lenin seems to have sensed that the entire philosophical heritage of positivism, both in its vulgarly materialist forms (for which he had a certain natural sympathy for but little philosophical agreement) and in the idealism of Mach, Avenarius, and Bogdanov (for which he had no sympathy whatsoever), were ultimately all products of a bourgeois society more concerned with self–preservation than social revolution. Hence, his fierce attack upon Machism, and his relatively gentle treatment of Haeckel and other materialists, merely represents a tactical political decision rather than a final philosophical judgment. In the last instance, both this vulgar materialism and Machist idealism were the offspring of a common parent, positivism, whose philosophical limitations reflected not only the blindness but also the self–interest of the bourgeois capitalist society which had produced them. And, in his rejection of Machism, we can see in Lenin a rejection (however subtle) of the bourgeois problematic which has produced not only the mystifications of Mach and Avenarius but also the philosophical vulgarities of Büchner, Haeckel, and, ultimately, Dietzgen as well.

It was this philosophical impasse, which appeared both natural and inescapable to most contemporary philosophers, that Pannekoek and Lenin confronted at the start of their careers as Marxist philosophers. Husserl, perhaps the only figure of that pivotal decade who managed to escape this dilemma and whose influence would be felt throughout the coming century, received no notice at the time in Marxist circles (or most others). On the other hand, those thinkers who dominated the debates of the time are now forgotten, although a reader unfamiliar with twentieth century philosophy would never suspect from reading Pannekoek that their prominence was fleeting and their subsequent influence (with minor exception of Mach on Logical Positivism) practically nil. Almost all would be swept away in the first two decades of the next century leaving scarcely a trace, as the rise of Phenomenology and Logical Positivism revealed the amateur status of these once–dominant figures in European philosophy.

Of course, things were hardly so clear at the time as they are now. While it is impossible to read *Materialism and Empirio–criticism* now without being struck by the utter obscurity of Lenin's opponents and their ideas, a quick glance at the books and journals of the period reveals how prominent these men were and how successfully their ideas infiltrated almost every aspect of philosophical discourse (not unlike post–modernism in our own time). It is difficult today to appreciate the foresight and courage involved in Lenin's dismissal of them. As Louis Althusser observed: "Lenin denounces and knocks down all these ephemerally philosophical scientists who thought their time had come. What is left of these characters today? We must concede at least that this philosophical ignoramus Lenin had good judgement."[39] A good judgment, it must also be admitted, that Pannekoek did not share. This historical myopia on Pannekoek's part is not simply a matter of bad luck or poor historiography. Rather, it reveals the extent to which Pannekoek's Marxism was intimately shaped by the post–positivist heritage of German philosophy. At the same time, contrary to both Lenin and his Soviet followers, Pannekoek's blindness was not a moral failure either, but only the philosophical one of a thinker who, like most in any era, was more captive to the prejudices and assumptions of his age than he ever realized. But if Pannekoek never escaped the conceptual categories of this earlier generation of thinkers, Lenin did—or at least began to do so. Lenin's *Materialism and Empirio–criticism*, despite its many failings, points a way out of the blind alley into which German philosophy had stumbled, and in doing so helped prepare the way not only for Soviet Marxism but also for much of Western Marxism as well.

(A) Pannekoek

A full discussion of Pannekoek's long and varied intellectual career—not to mention his political one—is beyond the scope of this introduction and is, in any case, available elsewhere.[40] Moreover, while his political alliance with and eventual schism from Lenin and Leninism are of interest from both a historical and biographical perspective, neither is essential to understanding his critique of Lenin (although they do add some psychological insight into the sources of Pannekoek's opposition to him). Even his development of Council communism, which is Pannekoek's greatest claim to fame within the Marxist tradition, adds nothing to the strength of his philosophical arguments. In order to assess his critique of Lenin, what is needed is an analysis (however brief) of the main conceptual pillars of Pannekoek's Marxism, which finds perhaps its last and fullest expression in his *Lenin as Philosopher* in 1938. When this is done, it will be clear that his commitment to a defective and essentially positivist version of dialectical materialism vitiates both his own philosophical achievement and his harsh criticism of Lenin.

Any understanding of Pannekoek's Marxism must begin the fact that his academic training and professional life was spent in the field of astronomy, to which he had already begun to make important contributions before his first encounter with Marx's thought in 1898 while a twenty–five year old doctoral student in Astronomy at the University of Leiden. There, the dominance of positivism within scientific circles of the 1890s influenced Pannekoek deeply, albeit possibly unconsciously, and helped determine many of his philosophical and historiographical decisions in *Lenin as Philosopher*.[41] Indeed, while Z. A. Jordan and Ludwig von Mises have questioned the importance of positivism for the social sciences in Germany during the late nineteenth century, its pervasive influence in the physical sciences where Pannekoek worked is almost universally acknowledged.[42] Thus, long before he had read or perhaps even heard of Marx, Pannekoek was already being formed by the positivist tradition which he later claimed to disown.[43]

If the philosophical foundations of his scientific training are the ultimate cause of Pannekoek's reversion to positivism, his enthusiasm for the thought of Joseph Dietzgen is surely the proximate cause. Indeed, perhaps the decisive event of this period of Pannekoek's intellectual life, equal to his conversion to Marxism, was the discovery by him of the writings of Dietzgen and their concern with the implications of Marxist philosophy for scientific theory. He wrote of this discovery:

> Here I found for the first time everything that I had been looking for: a clear, systematic elaboration of a theory of knowledge and an analysis of the nature of concepts and abstractions. . . . Through this reading I was able to completely clarify my conception of the underlying relationship between Marxism and epistemology and develop it into a unified whole.[44]

Disregarding the reservations of Marx and Engels concerning Dietzgen's philosophical competence—reservations shared and amplified by Lenin—Pannekoek accepted at face value the self–description of Dietzgen's system as dialectical and made it his own. Not surprisingly, this initial dependence manifested itself in Pannekoek's tendency to repeat rather than critique or develop Dietzgen's understanding of dialectics, epistemology, and materialism.

Like Dietzgen before him, Pannekoek presents the dialectic not as a process in the material world but rather as an activity of the individual thinking subject in her attempt to adequately conceptualize the world:

> Dialectical thinking is adequate to reality in that in handling the concepts it is aware that the finite cannot render the infinite, nor the static the dynamic, and that every concept has to develop into new concepts, even into its opposite. Metaphysical, undialectical thinking, on the other hand, leads to dogmatic assertions and contradictions because it views conceptions formed by thought as fixed, independent entities that make up the reality of the world.[45]

Again following Dietzgen's example, Pannekoek allowed this rather sloganeered presentation of dialectical thinking to serve more as an assault weapon against his opponents than as a tool for philosophical reflection. His verbal commitment to the necessity of "dialectical thinking", though, cannot mask the ambiguity and confusion in Pannekoek's understanding of the dialectic. What pattern of development or unfolding does it follow? What exactly is the relationship between concepts and the objects they represent? These questions are never seriously asked by Pannekoek.

Ultimately, though, Pannekoek never needed to ask them, since the dialectic never really informed his practice either as a Marxist or as a scientist. Once any concrete investigation of the world began, Pannekoek immediately adopted both the methods and conceptual categories of scientific positivism as essentially adequate and correct. Despite his admission that "natural scientists form a part of middle–class society; they are in continual contact with the bourgeoisie and are influenced by its spiritual trends,"[46] Pannekoek exempts the concept systems of the physical sciences from the sort of searching ideological critique which Marx had given to classical political economy:

> Natural science proper, surely, does not suffer from this shortcoming [of metaphysical thinking]. It surmounts difficulties and contradictions in practice insofar as continually it revises its

formulations, increases their richness by going into finer details, improves the qualitative distinctions by mathematical formulas, completes them by additions and corrections, thereby bringing the picture ever closer to the original, the world of phenomena. The lack of dialectical reasoning becomes disturbing only when the scientist passes from his special field of knowledge towards general philosophical reasonings, as is the case with middle–class materialism.[47]

This privileging of science as an intellectual discipline largely immune in its day to day activities from the contamination of bourgeois ideology, while supported by Dietzgen's writings, cannot be found in the writings of Marx and certainly does not reflect a dialectical pattern of thinking. Rather, it is completely positivist in origin and character.

Pannekoek never challenged the positivist foundations of modern science, and instead focused his criticisms only on its role as a support of modern capitalism. John Gerber neatly summarizes these conservative views about science, despite any concerns Pannekoek may have had about its role in the development and maintenance of capitalism:

> But such a conception of science as "class science" [which Pannekoek occasionally advanced] did not entail the view that every class maintains its own special set of scientific views, but "that a certain form of science can be both an object and a weapon of class struggle, and that a class has an interest only in the investigation and diffusion of those truths which directly advance its own living conditions.[48]

This uncritical stance towards the conceptual foundations of science in Pannekoek's philosophy is essentially a repetition of the traditional nineteenth century understanding of scientific progress as linear and continuous and of its findings as objectively true in the classical sense. Any concerns about the hegemony of the bourgeoisie over scientific inquiry and the scientific ideology of modern society, such as Antonio Gramsci might have voiced, or a recognition that scientific concept formation always occurs within a class–based society and reflects its prejudices, as Lukacs argued, are absent here.[49] That Pannekoek in his philosophy always operated within a conceptual realm defined by nineteenth century positivism rather than Marx becomes clearer still in his endorsement and defense of Mach's empiricist theory of knowledge. He writes: "Mach's thesis that the world consists only of our sensations expresses the truth that we know of the world only through our sensations; they are the materials out of which we build our world; in this sense the world, including myself, 'consists' of sensations only."[50] Nor did his commitment to empiricism end with Mach. Even after discussing and criticizing the Logical Positivism of so "bourgeois" a philosopher as Rudolf Carnap, Pannekoek's final judgment on the inadequacies of positivist epistemology consists not in a radical attack upon its philosophical foundations but only in a criticism of its sufficiency as a world–view: "It is easy to see the limitedness of this world structure [of Mach and Logical Positivism]. It is not finished. The world thus constituted by Mach and Carnap is a momentary world supposed unchanging. The fact that the world is in continuous evolution is disregarded. *So we must go past where Carnap stopped.* [emphasis added]"[51] But to do so, of course, entails following Mach and Carnap so far as they went, namely, the acceptance of an empiricist and positivist epistemology within which "dialectical thinking" is nothing more than an open–minded attitude towards particular scientific theories which never challenges the positivist and supposedly "objective" character of modern scientific practice.

It is only when Mach converts his epistemological idealism into an ontological one that Pannekoek parts company with him, and in general he dismisses these moves by Mach as unjustified—indeed, as symptomatic of a mystifying trend in bourgeois thought: "Mach's tendency to emphasize the subjective side of experience appears in that the immediately given elements of the world, which we call phenomena, are denoted as sensations."[52] As a Marxist and a materialist, Pannekoek had no choice but to reject this move, even while accepting Mach's premises in making it, and to suggest that a proper Marxist analysis of the function of philosophy within the class struggle could prevent such a mistake. Hence, Pannekoek can praise Dietzgen for sharing Mach's basic philosophical assumptions and methods while drawing materialist rather than idealist conclusions:

> The similarity here [between Mach and Dietzgen's epistemology] is manifest. The differences are accounted for by their different class views. Dietzgen stood on the basis of dialectical materialism, and his expositions were a direct consequence of Marxism. Mach, borne by the incipient reaction of the bourgeoisie, saw his task in a fundamental criticism of physical materialism by asserting dominance to some spiritual principle.[53]

Pannekoek's own rejection of Machist idealism and his embrace of materialism is clear enough when he writes that "when now man is building up the world out of his sensations, it is a reconstruction in the mind of an already objectively existing world." [See below, p. 110.—Editor]

Having affirmed materialism, though, Pannekoek then advances a version of it which was much closer on a metaphysical level to that of Büchner and Moleschott than to that of Marx. He writes:

> The world is the totality of an infinite number of parts acting upon another; every part consists in its totality of its actions and reactions with the rest, and all these mutual actions are the phenomena, the object of science. Man is also part of the world; we too are the totality of our mutual interactions with the rest, the outer world.[54]

This version of monistic materialism, while perhaps capable of a dialectical interpretation, is never given one by Pannekoek. Rather, the model of interaction between the different "parts" of the world is, for Pannekoek, a mechanistic and not a dialectical one. This is made clear, ironically, in his efforts to distance himself from the sorts of vulgar materialism discussed earlier:

> "Man is a link in the chain of cause and effect; necessity in social development is a necessity achieved by means of human action. The material world acts upon man, determines his consciousness, his ideas, his will, his actions; so he reacts upon the world and changes it." This is poles apart from the "mechanistic materialism" which "assumes that our thoughts are determined by the motion of

atoms in the cells of our brains. Marxism considers our thoughts to be determined by our social experience observed through the senses or felt as direct bodily needs."[55]

Both because of his own inadequate training in philosophy and because of the pernicious influence of Dietzgen, Pannekoek never realizes that the simple belief that mechanistic causality runs both towards and from the human organism is a very far cry from the dialectic as Hegel, Marx, and even Engels had understood it.

This fundamentally undialectical understanding of existence is further revealed in Pannekoek's subtle but unmistakable reduction of Marx's theory of human praxis, according to which man and the natural world are essentially interdependent for their being, to a much more tame and ontologically unimaginative instrumentalism wherein human activity develops and partially conceals the independently existing material substratum of nature. Pannekoek writes:

> Man does not stand against nature as to an external alien world. By the toil of his hands man transforms the world, to such an extent that the original natural substance is hardly discernible, and in this process transforms himself too. Thus man himself builds his new world: human society, imbedded in nature transformed into a technical apparatus.[56]

Whatever its philosophical merits, this cannot be considered a dialectical or Marxist theory of materialism. One does not become a Marxist by claiming that "man with his brain and mind is intimately connected with the rest of the animal kingdom and the inorganic world," which is neither a novel nor uniquely Marxist insight.[57]

One need only compare Pannekoek's text with the Marx's *Economic and Political Manuscripts* of 1844 to see how far down the road towards positivism Pannekoek's materialism has traveled and how far away from Marx's much more sophisticated and, for lack of a better term, Hegelian notion of nature wherein not only the activities but the very existence of both the human and the natural orders are essentially connected to one another. There Marx writes:

> But nature too, taken abstractly, for itself—nature fixed in isola-
> tion from man—is nothing for man. . . . Nature as nature—that is
> to say, insofar as it is sensuously distinguished from that secret sense
> hidden within it—nature isolated, distinguished from these ab-
> stractions, is nothing —a nothing proving itself to be nothing—is
> devoid of sense, or has only the sense of being an externality which
> has to be annulled.[58]

This understanding of nature is radically different from Pannekoek's
vision of an objectively present (in the Heideggerian sense) natural
order within which the human and the natural may well co–exist
and interact but never interpenetrate one another.

The end result of this understanding of materialism is to subordinate the human sciences to the natural ones, and the human order to
the natural one, in direct contradiction of Marx's rejection of a "pure"
and inhuman nature. As a result, the theories of Marx, far from providing a governing framework within which to critique and judge all
other sciences and philosophies, became for Pannekoek a "regional"
science of social development as practically autonomous and as theoretically dependent as biology, chemistry, psychology, or any other
science of the era. As Gerber writes: "Although the new 'spiritual
science' of Marxism was linked with the bourgeois scientific meth-
odologies of the past through the process of social and historical development, Pannekoek's fundamental distinction between social and
natural science ruled out any connection between Marxism and physical theory."[59] In other words, there could never be for Pannekoek a
distinctively marxist metaphysic, but only a natural scientific one
within which the human sciences could and must be fitted and justi-
fied.

Ultimately, Pannekoek's philosophical eclecticism resulted not in a
transcendence or resolution of the philosophical problems of late
nineteenth century German philosophy but rather in their repetition within a nominally Marxist framework. The authority of bourgeois science, both in its commitment to a vulgar and mechanistic
materialism and to an empiricist epistemology, always trumped any
efforts of Marxism to critique its intellectual foundations. Certainly,
we find in Pannekoek's writings criticisms of particular thinkers and
particular theories, oftentimes in the name of Marxist theory or prac-

tice. What is always absent, though, is a distinctively Marxist philosophical framework which can not only accommodate but can also delimit the claims to objectivity and scientificity of bourgeois culture. Rather, Pannekoek is always put in the awkward position (for a Marxist) of admitting the ultimate and unimpeachable truth of bourgeois science while at the same time demanding a revolutionary political practice which would overthrow the very society which those sciences operate within and for which they provide theoretical support.

In fairness to Pannekoek, and without intending to soften the harsh criticisms made of him as a philosopher and critic of Lenin, the intellectual and moral strengths which he exhibited during his lifetime should be acknowledged, if for no other reason than to avoid the Leninist tendency to equate intellectual or political errors with moral terpitude. In *Lenin as Philosopher*, Pannekoek did attempt to give a relatively fair and even–handed account of the philosophical backdrop to Lenin's thought, something few Western Marxists would bother and few Soviet Marxists would dare to do in the twentieth century. For this alone, and despite the many weaknesses of his historical reconstruction which this introduction has tried to remedy, his work deserves attention. In addition, Pannekoek helped to sustain (though perhaps without being aware of it) the important philosophical dialogue between scientific positivism and the Marxist tradition which had dominated the era of the Second International during a period in which very few thinkers, East or West, saw it as important. In that way, his thought, including his criticisms of Lenin, can still serve as a small bridge between more recent attempts of Analytic Marxism and the classical foundations of Orthodox Marxism. Whatever one's estimation of Analytic Marxism, the need for diversity and intellectual daring in Marxist philosophy at the beginning of a new century cannot be seriously questioned. Likewise, the connections which Pannekoek saw between his own philosophical work and the foundations of Council communism, and the courage this work gave him to continue struggling for Communism and against Soviet Marxism during the darkest years of Stalinism, certainly demands respect and should illicit more than a little interest during our own time.

In the final analysis, though, one searching for a solution to or an escape from the philosophical world which both was produced by and supported the bourgeoisie of the nineteenth century needs to look elsewhere than Pannekoek's thought. Proceeding along philosophical lines laid down not by Marx but by the middle–class scientists under whom he studied, Pannekoek's philosophical accomplishment, much like Dietzgen's before him, never went beyond and almost certainly died along with the passing of that class and their historical era. Contrary to Pannekoek's arguments, it is in fact Lenin who first began (however haltingly) to strike a new path for Marxist philosophy in his *Materialism and Empirio–criticism* in 1908.

(B) Lenin

Despite the wealth of studies by both enthusiasts and demonizers over the last three–quarters century, no definitive account of Lenin's philosophical writings has yet appeared nor, for a variety of historical and political reasons, is one likely in the foreseeable future.[60] Given this, and the limitations both of format and authorial ability, it should not be surprising that an exhaustive or even an adequate discussion of Lenin's philosophical system (if indeed his writings deserve such a name, which is doubtful) cannot be given here. The more modest goal of this introduction is only to indicate briefly the way in which two main features of Lenin's *Materialism and Empirio–criticism*, namely, his infamous "copy theory" of knowledge and his understanding of materialism, far from being either pre–critical or uncritical, are in fact significant philosophical responses to and advances beyond the post–positivist philosophical systems of his day. This alone is sufficient to distinguish Lenin from his philosophical predecessors and to suggest the continuing interest and potential of even his earliest philosophical writings.

Curiously, Lenin's main attempt to transcend the problematic of post–positivist philosophy can be found in the most universally reviled part of his philosophy, namely, his copy theory of knowledge, which he saw both as the necessary epistemological counterpart of any materialism and the only possible route out of the agnosticism and idealism of his opponents. In *Materialism and Empirio–criticism* Lenin charges that the idealism and agnosticism which characterized not only of the Russian Machists whom he fought but also Berkeley and Kant before them (and, as it turned out, the Logicial Positivists who followed) was the result of an even more fundamental and erroneous philosophical decision by all of them to adopt an empiricist epistemology. The empiricist belief that our knowledge of the world is constructed out of a field of sense–data immediately present to consciousness (e.g., Hume's "impressions" or Mach's "world–elements") resulted in this sense–data becoming an insuperable barrier between human consciousness and the external world. In turn, this belief that our access to the external world is forever mediated by this screen of sensations produced a whole host of skeptical problems about the existence and nature of that world which had preoccupied much of eighteenth and nineteenth century philosophy.

The first historical example of this skepticism (although Lenin fails to point out that its roots can be found in both Descartes and Locke) is found in the idealism of Berkeley, who, according to Lenin, "denies 'only' the teaching of the philosophers, viz., the theory of knowledge, which seriously and resolutely takes as the foundation of all its reasoning the recognition of the external world and the reflection thereof in the minds of men."[61] Once the source of knowledge ceased to be objects in the world and instead became the sense–impressions "caused" by these objects in the knowing subject, the inevitable result was either an idealism which cut through these skeptical problems by denying the existence of the external world, as Berkeley did, or an agnosticism which functioned as a *de facto* idealism by its silence about the reality of the world outside the mind, as was the case with Hume. In both cases, the underlying problem was an epistemology that "regards sensation as being not the connection between consciousness and the external world, but a fence, a wall, separating consciousness from the external world—not an image of the external world phenomenon corresponding to the sensation, but as the 'sole entity.'"[62] Lenin makes it clear at the beginning of *Materialism and Empirio–criticism* that, in his opinion, the theories of Bogdanov and Lunacharsky are nothing but a repetition of the same *empiricist cum idealist* mistakes Berkeley had made some two centuries earlier.

This attack by Lenin on the historical foundation of his opponents' theories, his initial decision to trace the empirio–critical movement back to Berkeley and Hume rather than just to Mach, should be seen not simply a polemical device to tie them to unpopular figures. Rather, it reflects a philosophical judgment about the epistemological failures of classical empiricism in general, both in its early eighteenth century and late nineteenth century varieties. Accordingly, Lenin saw the choice between *any* version of empiricism and the copy theory of knowledge as perhaps the fundamental decision for any philosopher, but especially for a Marxist one. Even Plekhanov's theory of knowledge, according to which our ideas are "symbols" or "hieroglyphs" of the external world, fails Lenin's epistemological test. As a result of this error, and despite his impeccable Marxist and materialist credentials, Plekhanov's writings had been employed to support the empirio–critical position: "For instance, our Machist would–be Marxists fastened with glee on Plekhanov's 'hieroglyphs', that is, on the theory that man's sensations and ideas are not copies of real things and processes of nature, not their images, but conventional signs, symbols, hieroglyphs, and so on."[63] For Lenin, there could only be one scientifically and politically reliable assumption about the nature of knowledge, namely, that "sensation is indeed the direct connection between consciousness and the external world."[64] It is in order to explain this "direct connection" that he introduces the copy theory of knowledge.

Siding with Marx and Engels against this empiricist tradition, of which positivism, Machism, and Empirio–criticism were only the latest manifestations, Lenin argues that our knowledge is in fact a "copy" or "reflection" or "reproduction" or "photograph" (he varies his terminology from place to place) of the external world, or that "our sensation, our consciousness is only *an image* of the external world."[65] Lenin traces this theory back to Engels (whose agreement with Marx on all philosophical questions he takes for granted), who "constantly and without exception speaks in his works of things and their mental pictures or images, and it is obvious that these mental images arise exclusively from sensations."[66] No detailed discussion of exactly how mental images copy or reproduce physical objects is given by Lenin, nor does he raise or answer traditional objections to what can only be called a version of "naive realism" (although, as he rather unhelpfully explains, "naive realism" is actually only the common–sense assumption of an independently existing world known by the mind, and therefore is not a term of abuse but a recognition of mental health).[67]

Not surprisingly, Lenin's defense of the copy theory of knowledge has drawn extensive criticism among English–speaking philosophers, especially during the heyday of Logical Positivism, in large part because of the immediate objections to it which can be raised from within the empiricist problematic which governed almost all Anglo–American philosophy in the twentieth century. Much like Husserl, Heidegger, and the overwhelming majority of continental thinkers since them, Lenin has had great difficulty receiving a serious hearing in many English–speaking quarters, a situation hardly helped by the generally dismal level of Soviet commentary and criticism made available in the West (or, so far as that goes, left untranslated from the Russian).[68] Even those who did consider his theory, even in passing, usually believed themselves to have refuted it by mentioning bent sticks in water or square towers seen at a distance. Only rarely have non–Marxist philosophers attempted an even–handed and sophisticated critique of his thought.[69]

Especially when one considers the frequency with which his thought is dismissed as "pre–critical" or "amateurish", what is most remarkable about Lenin's copy theory is the manner in which he consciously and intentionally operates outside the parameters of empiricism accepted by the positivist and post–positivist philosophers of his era (as well as by Pannekoek). Lenin immediately rejects the empiricist view that our knowledge is of discrete *sensibilia* capable of a variety of different combinations whose interconnections must be provided by the mind based on some arbitrary principle (e.g., scientific convenience for Mach, or class–specific ideological structures for Bogdanov). In contrast, Lenin's copy theory is remarkably "holistic" (for lack of a better term) in its portrayal of how our minds represent the external world. He argues that our knowledge is of real *objects* in nature and reflects real *connections* between these objects, not that it constructs these objects and the connections between them out of raw sense–data. Keeping his focus on the essential philosophical questions at hand, Lenin does not allow himself to be drawn off target by debates over the particular adequacy of one or the other empiricist theories of knowledge for scientific description of natural events (admitting thereby the practical adequacy of empiricism for science without ceding its theoretical correctness). He writes:

> The really important epistemological question that divides the philosophical trends is not the degree of precision attained by our descriptions of causal connections, or whether these descriptions can be expressed in exact mathematical formulas, but whether the source of our knowledge of these connections is objective natural law or properties of our mind, its innate faculty of apprehending certain *a priori* truths, and so forth.[70]

The question, in short, is whether our ideas correspond (a term noticeably left undefined) to real features of the external world and are reliable copies of these, or whether the mind instead is the author and cause of this external world. For Lenin, any other presentation of the question misses the fundamental challenge which empiricism poses both to Marxism and materialism.

Of course, Lenin never claims that, as a result of the copy theory of knowledge, we have indubitable knowledge of the world or that error and imprecision cannot occur in our knowing. He does occasionally let his polemic drive him to more extreme formulations of the copy theory, going so far as to claim that "the laws of thought reflect the forms of actual existence of objects, fully resemble and do not differ from these forms."[71] However, such exaggerations are exceptions to the rule. The accusation made against Lenin that his thought is "pre–critical" (a term Althusser uses approvingly) is not only unfair but also misses the point of his efforts in *Materialism and Empirio–criticism*, namely, to escape the entire problematic of modern epistemology which, he believes, results inevitably in skepticism or idealism:

> It is beyond doubt that an image can never wholly compare with the model, but an image is one thing, a symbol, a *conventional sign*, another. The image inevitably and of necessity implies the objective reality of that which it 'images.' 'Conventional sign', symbol,

hieroglyph are concepts which introduce an entirely unnecessary element of agnosticism.[72]

In this respect, Lenin's philosophy is not so much pre–critical as it is pre–Cartesian in its concerns. Confronted with the possibility of a radical relativism (under the guise of Machist idealism or scientific conventionalism) which would call into question the scientific character of Marxism, his goal in using the copy theory is to remove any ground for *systematically* raising skeptical objections against our knowledge–claims. He never denies that any particular idea may not accurately or adequately correspond to its object.

On the other hand, since the objects known by the mind and the relationships between them reflect actually existing objects and relationships, no imprecision or error in our knowledge can be removed by a "reconfiguration" of sense–data into a more self–consistent combination, as had been attempted by the Machists when confronted with the failure of traditional physics. Lenin claims that these efforts can only lead not to scientific advance but to the undermining of any scientific truth whatsoever:

> Hence, in its philosophical aspect, the essence of the 'crisis in modern physics' is that the old physics regarded its theories as 'real knowledge of the material world', i.e., a reflection of objective reality. The new trend in physics regards theories only as symbols, signs, and marks for practice, i.e., it denies the existence of an objective reality independent of our mind and reflected by it.[73]

Far from being a possible solution to problems of modern science, Lenin says, radical empiricism is the main cause, since it renders any final adjudication of scientific controversy impossible by denying the independent existence of an objective world. The essential question concerning any scientific theory, such as those concerning space and time, is whether

> our relative ideas of space and time [are] approximations to objectively real forms of being; or are they only products of the developing, organising, harmonising, etc., human mind? This and this alone is the basic epistemological problem on which the truly fundamental philosophical trends are divided.[74]

But, having admitted that our images or ideas of objects may be imprecise or "relative", how does Lenin suggest such imperfections be identified and removed from our understanding? Against these empiricist efforts at a conceptual or ideological solution to the problem of knowledge, Lenin argues that the only possible correction to error must be found in actual (or as Marx would say, sensuous) human practice:

> The mastery of nature manifested in human practice is a result of an objectively correct reflection within the human head of the phenomena and processes of nature, and is proof of the fact that this reflection (within the limits of what is revealed by practice) is objective, eternal, absolute truth.[75]

Commenting elsewhere on Marx's theses on Feuerbach, Lenin observes that "the 'objective truth' of thinking means *nothing else* than the *existence* of objects ('things–in–themselves') *truly* reflected by thinking."[76] Unfortunately, in *Materialism and Empirio–criticism* Lenin never develops this theory of praxis and its relationship to knowledge beyond the rather pedestrian interpretation of Marx given above. Nor are we helped by his claim that "[O]ur perceptions and ideas are images. Verification of these images, differentiation between true and false images, is given by practice."[77] The obvious commitment to materialism in the text gives some help, or at least rules out certain interpretations, but even then (as was the case with Marx's views) a wide range of possible interpretations remains without any real guidance from Lenin on which to follow. Ultimately, despite its solid Marxist credentials, Lenin's statements on the role of praxis in epistemology raises as many questions as it answers.

Nor is this the only problem which can be raised with Lenin's theory of knowledge. David Bakhurst discusses at length the tension between the subject–object dualism which such a theory demands (i.e., ideas belong to a metaphysical subject corresponding to objects outside the subject) and Lenin's equally fierce opposition to any non–materialist ontology of consciousness which might make help make sense out of what exactly these ideas are or how they resemble objects outside the mind. Bakhurst even suggests that the copy or reflection theory of knowledge Lenin maintains in *Materialism and Empirio–criticism* constitutes a serious barrier to Lenin's otherwise vigorous attempts to reconcile a materialist and realist theory of knowledge with a purely materialist ontology. He writes:

> All that stands between Lenin and radical realism [that is, the belief that ideas simply "are" the objects of knowledge belonging to the sensuous human agent as part of his existence in the world] is reflection theory. Surely, there must be some reading of the view that minds 'reflect' reality that does not entail representative realism. However, to force such a reading on Lenin would be artificial.[78]

David–Hillel Ruben, confronting the same problem, suggests that Plekhanov's "symbolic" intepretation of ideas can oversome such problems by removing visual content from mental images and instead making them mere devices for correlating various practices, thereby also allowing us to avoid the subject–object dualism which any representational or pictorial theory of ideas is in danger of falling into.[79] But this solution, whatever its philosophical attractions, has to overcome Lenin's explicit rejection of Plekhanov's theory as incompatible with Marxist political practice, a topic Ruben passes over in silence. While these suggestions are very promising as possible paths for developing Marxist philosophy (paths Bakhurst claims were further mapped out by Evald Ilyenkov in the Soviet Union), they clearly move well beyond either the text or the intentions of Lenin. And, while perhaps a future Marxist epistemology might need to develop just the sort of radically materialist anthropology which Bakhurst hints at in order to move beyond both empiricism *and* Lenin's copy–theory, such a task lies outside the boundaries of this discussion.

Still, Bakhurst is certainly correct in seeing an important philosophical connection (even if it is problematical) between Lenin's copy theory of knowledge and his commitment to a strictly materialist ontology. Lenin repeatedly makes the linkage himself in *Materialism and Empirio–criticism*, portraying the copy theory as the epistemological counterpart of an authentic materialism: "Our sensation, our consciousness is only *an image* of the external world, and it is obvious that the image cannot exist without the thing imaged, and that the latter exists independently of that which images it. Materialism *deliberately* make the 'naive' belief of mankind the foundation of its theory of knowledge."[80] Elsewhere he is even more direct in this identification: "The recognition of theory as a copy, as an approximate copy of objective reality, is materialism."[81] But what exactly does Lenin mean in his identification of realism and materialism? In answering this, we will see the way in which Lenin, having moved beyond the epistemology of the positivist tradition, also breaks with its understanding of materialism. He does this, not by choosing between epistemology and ontology, as had the materialists and idealists of previous generations, but by attempting to unite them.

First, however, it needs to be made clear in what respect Lenin's materialism is not at all original, indeed, in what respect it is almost painfully derivative and inadequate. As Bakhurst has already suggested, Lenin's attempt to explain human consciousness as the result of material processes in the brain is a necessary counterpart of his rejection of subject–object dualism, and requires a new method of conceptualizing mental life which breaks out of the dualism which gave rise to modern empiricism. Unfortunately, what we find in *Materialism and Empirio–criticism* is nothing more than a repetition of the biological materialism which Büchner, Moleschott and others had put forward without success half a century earlier, in which it is simply assumed that a physical account of brain processes can be substituted for the concept of the mental without difficulty or remainder. A representative example of these attempts reads:

> This is materialism: matter acting upon our sense–organs produces sensations. Sensation depends upon the brain, nerves, retina, etc., i.e., on matter organised in a definite way. The existence of matter does not depend on sensation. Matter is primary. Sensation, thought, consciousness are the supreme product of matter organised in a particular way. Such are the views of materialism in general, and of Marx and Engels in particular.[82]

Whatever the intrinsic merit or even necessity for Marxist philosophy of a reductive materialist account of consciousness, this repetition of the old metaphysical materialism from the eighteenth and nineteenth centuries clearly won't suffice. And, while it is to be expected that Lenin, in his first major foray into metaphysics, would not immediately resolve all the problems which troubled Marxist philosophy, pretending that his attempted resolution of the mind–body problem marks any advance over previous efforts is useless. While he does perhaps begin to make a little headway in moving beyond this problem in his *Philosophical Notebooks* in 1916, the same cannot be said of *Materialism and Empirio–criticism* in 1908.[83]

Although his rather facile attempt at a reductive materialist theory of mind has been widely criticised, it should not distract us from the original and very suggestive account of materialism also found in *Materialism and Empirio–criticism*. Lenin's chief interest in materialism in this early work is quite clearly not defined by the traditional mind–body problem but rather by the skeptical and idealist tendencies about the external world raised by the empiricist tradition which dominates modern science. Since the copy theory by definition entails the existence of a world outside of consciousness which is being copied, Lenin conceives materialism as the ontological correlate of his epistemology: "Materialism is the recognition of 'objects in themselves', or outside the mind; ideas and sensations are copies or images of those objects. The opposite doctrine (idealism) claims that objects do not exist 'without the mind; objects are 'combinations of sensations.'"[84] Elsewhere, Lenin is even more explicit in his equation of materialism and realism:

> Let us note that the term realism is here employed as the antithesis of idealism. Following Engels, I use *only* the term materialism in this sense, and consider it the sole correct terminology, especially since the term 'realism' has been bedraggled by the positivists and other muddleheads who oscillate between materialism and idealism.[85]

On the surface, it seems odd that Lenin would define his materialism around an epistemological rather than a scientific problematic, especially since Marx had shown so little interest in epistemology in his own writings, famously dismissing such questions as "scholasticism" in his Theses on Feuerbach. Indeed, Marx never felt the need to develop a distinct philosophy of science and accepted the scientific discoveries of his day as fundamentally compatible with his own materialist world view. However, after his death in 1883 science underwent a crisis which prevented Lenin from either assuming that the physical sciences automatically provided support for Marxist theory or, the next best thing, passing the question over in silence. Since the time of Engels, the last great theorist of Marxism, the problem of matter had acquired fundamental significance in the natural sciences. In the days of Marx and Engels the concept of matter had appeared exceptionally simple, illuminating, and clear. Science considered itself to have found, in the atom, the essential nature of matter. But the discovery of radio–activity in certain elements during the closing years of the previous century had compelled the assumption that the atom did not represent the utmost limit of divisibility in matter. . . . At this point the concept of the atom, previously so clear, had become distinctly obscure. Hence it came about that people had begun to talk of a crisis in physics, of the 'ruin' of the old principles (Henri Poincaré), of the 'dematerialization of the atom' and of the 'disappearance of matter.'[86]

Lenin, always well read if nothing else, was familiar with this crisis within science and the challenge it posed for materialism. He writes:

> The *essence* of the crisis in modern physics consists in the break–down of the old laws and basic principles, in the rejection of an objective reality existing outside the mind, that is, in the replacement of materialism by idealism and agnosticism. 'Matter has disappeared'—one may thus express the fundamental and characteristic difficulty in relation to many particular questions which has created this crisis.[87]

In fact, it was Mach's ability to accommodate idealist and anti–realist theories of science (as shown by his occasional denial of the extra–theoretical existence of sub–atomic particles mentioned above) which had placed him in the forefront of scientific theory from the 1880s onwards and which made him such an attractive thinker to thinkers such as Bogdanov who were attempting to update Marxist theory in light of these new developments in science.

Lenin's response to this attempt to renovate Marxism was to challenge the underlying assumption that philosophically significant changes had taken place in science such as would require any changes in Marxist theory: "But we are concerned *now* not with theories of physics but with a fundamental philosophical problem."[88] While admitting that very important developments had occurred within physics, Lenin argued that it is

> absolutely unpardonable to confuse, as the Machists do, any particular theory of the structure of matter with the epistemological category, to confuse the problem of the new properties of new aspects of matter (electrons, for example) with the old problem of the theory of knowledge, with the problem of the sources of our knowledge, the existence of objective truth, etc.[89]

In effect, Lenin is responding to the revolution which occurred in modern physics around the turn of the last century and the challenge it posed to traditional materialism by separating out the scientific and theory–laden features of it (which Marx had never needed or bothered to do) and retaining only the philosophical content of it. The result is a conception of matter stripped of any specific theoretical content and instead assigned the philosophical task of guaranteeing the extra–mental reference of our mental concepts. He writes:

> Matter is a philosophical category denoting the objective reality which is given to man by his sensations, and which is copied, photographed and reflected by our sensations, while existing independently of them. Therefore, to say that such a concept can become 'antiquated' is *childish talk*, a senseless repetition of the arguments of fashionable *reactionary* philosophy.[90]

The various debates and changes of fashion within physics, however necessary they may be for the development of scientific theory, cannot undermine the Marxist belief in materialism, Lenin claims, since the *sole* 'property' of matter with whose recognition philosophical materialism is bound up is the property of *being an objective reality*, of existing outside the mind. . . . Thus, the question [of whether non–perceived physical entities such as electrons exist independent of the mind] is decided in favor of materialism, for the concept matter, as we already stated, epistemologically implies *nothing but* objective reality existing independently of the human mind and reflected by it.[91]

As with his theory of knowledge, Lenin's minimalist version of materialism is not without its problems. The most serious is that, with materialism as a philosophical thesis completely independent of any specific scientific theory, Lenin is in the very real danger of supporting rather than refuting his idealist opponents since he has no immediately obvious means of using this philosophical concept of matter as a means of verifying or falsifying specific scientific theories. That is, it is very unclear what role, if any, Lenin's materialism can play in everyday scientific practice, a problem compounded the absence of any explicit or adequate theory of praxis mentioned earlier. If materialism as a philosophical thesis is truly independent of the question whether Bohr or Lucretius correctly described the structure of matter, why is it not also independent of the question whether Bohr or Mach did so? G. A. Paul goes so far as to accuse Lenin's materialism of being "little more than a figure of speech."[92] While this may overstate the troubles with it, it is quite unclear exactly how his materialism could offer the sort of corrective to any errors in our scientific knowledge. It is just this role as corrective and limit to scientific concepts, though, that led Lenin to identify materialism and realism to begin with.

Nevertheless, Lenin's minimalist version of materialism clearly marks an advance over the earlier versions of Büchner and others, even in the absence of any clear answers to the problem raised above. At the very least, Lenin has correctly identified the need for Marxist philosophers to distinguish the philosophical function performed by materialism (e.g., a commitment to an external world independent of the knowing subject) from it scientific role in providing particular explanatory frameworks for natural phenomena. As the failures both of German positivism and Russian Machism show, this distinction between a philosophical and a scientific materialism, and their logical independence, was hardly obvious before Lenin's *Materialism and Empirio–criticism*. As was the case with his critique of empiricism and his defense of the copy theory of knowledge, even if this version of materialism raises a new set of problems both for scientists and philosophers, by cutting the Gordian know between scientific and philosophical materialism Lenin has at least opened up a *new* set of problems for Marxism to solve.

When we consider that it was written at the end of a long half–century of positivism, which had captured Pannekoek and almost all Lenin's contemporaries in its intellectual net, *Materialism and Empirio–criticism* reveals itself a significant and enduring philosophical achievement. Despite its problems, and a combative style which led more often to their being compounded by Lenin's exaggeration and smothering of all nuance, its ability to break free of these older forms of thought and point beyond the late nineteenth century philosophical tradition remains impressive some seventy–five years later. Last but not least, the potential for further Marxist philosophizing contained in these accomplishments gives a renewed interest to Pannekoek's *Lenin as Philosopher* as one of the key documents in the history of the interpretation of Lenin's thought, albeit one looking backwards most of the time. Taken together, they constitute a Janus–faced milestone in the history of Marxist thought.

Notes

[1] A generation ago, David McLellan, in his *Marxism after Marx* (New York: Harper and Row, 1979), still considered Pannekoek the leading interpreter of Lenin's philosophy His supplemental list of references (limited to the English literature) includes: G.A. Paul, "Lenin's Theory of Perception." *Analysis* 5, no. 5 (August 1938); David–Hillel Ruben, *Marxism and Materialism: A Study in Marxist Theory of Knowledge* (Sussex: Harvester Press, 1977), especially chaps. 4 and 5; Z. A. Jordan, "The Dialectical Materialism of Lenin," *Slavic Review* 25, no. 2 (1966). Jordan's article, in an expanded form, was incorporated into his *The Evolution of Dialectical Materialism* (New York: St. Martin's, 1967). Of these three authors, Ruben's discussion is both the most substantive and positive in its assessment of Lenin. Since Ruben's work, the most important discussion in English of *Materialism and Empirio–criticism* can be found in David Bakhurst, *Consciousness and Revolution in Soviet Philosophy from the Bolsheviks to Evald Ilyenkov* (Cambridge: Cambridge University Press, 1991).

Kevin Anderson's *Lenin, Hegel, and Western Marxism* (Chicago: University of Illinois Press, 1995) dismisses *Materialism and Empirio–criticism* because of its "well–deserved reputation for crudity and dogmatism" (19) in favor of the more hegelian *Philosophical Notebooks* of 1916, and sees the two as discontinuous. However, Sebastiano Timpanaro (*On Materialism* [London: NLB, 1979], 246–254) makes a compelling argument for the essential unity of these two very different works, despite the real development in Lenin's thought which occurs between them.

German–speaking scholars from both sides of the Berlin Wall produced several useful—but at times excessively orthodox—works on *Materialism and Empirio–criticism* during the Cold War. These include: Jacques Milhau and Robert Stiegerwald, »*Lenin und der Revisionismus in der Philosophie*« und »*Zeitgemäße Bemerkungen zu Lenins Festellung, daß der Neukantianismus die philosophische Grundlage des Revisionismus dei*« (Frankfurt am Main: Verlag Marxistische Blätter GMBH, 1975); Dieter Wettich, *Warum und wie Lenins philosophisches Hauptwerk entstand: Entstehung, Methodik und Rezeption von* »*Materialismus und Empiriokritizismus*« (Berlin: Dietz Verlag, 1985); G. Wilczek, *Die Erkenntnislehre Lenins* (Pfaffenhofen/Ilmgau: Verlag W. Ludwig, 1974).

[2]Georg Lukacs, *Lenin: A Study of the Unity of His Thought*, tr. Rodney Livingstone (Cambridge, Mass.: MIT Press, 1970). The political context within which Lukacs wrote this book, namely, his attempt to rehabilitate his reputation after the attacks of Deborin and Rudas upon his *History and Class Consciousness*, is well known. That this work is essentially political rather than philosophical in character is shown by the fact that Slavoj Zizek, in his essay "Georg Lukacs as the Philosopher of Leninism" (in Georg Lukacs, *A Defence of History and Class Consciousness*, trans. Esther Leslie [London: Verso, 2000], 151–182) can avoid any mention of it.

[3]Although Anderson's *Lenin, Hegel, and Western Marxism*, following up the work of Raya Dunayevskaya, does attempt such a connection of Lenin's *Philosophical Notebooks* of 1914–1915 with his policies and politics after the October Revolution, *Materialism and Empirio–criticism* is passed over with minimal comment..

[4]Karl Korsch, "Lenin's Philosophy," reprinted in Anton Pannekoek, *Lenin as Philosopher* (London: Merlin Press, 1975), 109–19, 12. In the Merlin edition, Paul Mattick is misidentified as the author of this essay.

[5]"Positivism," in *A Dictionary of Marxist Thought*, 2nd ed., Tom Bottomore, ed. (London: Blackwell, 1991).

[6]In its more explicitly Comtean forms, positivism employed the concept of matter in a considerably more "metaphysical" sense, wherein its innate capacity for development into more and more complex entities, and ultimately into conscious and historically conditioned human beings, was emphasized. In these versions, positivism quickly duplicated the speculative excesses which it was originally founded to overcome. However, while this semi–hegelianized version of materialism did influence a few thinkers (including, eventually, Haeckel), it was generally rejected as a throwback to idealism and did not become a characteristic feature of nineteenth century positivism.

[7]Naturally, the development and fortunes of positivism varied considerably across Europe during the course of the century. For instance, in England during the 1840s John Stuart Mill helped fuel a popular enthusiasm for positivism, with Herbert Spencer later taking up its cause when Mill became disenchanted with Comte's increasingly messianic understanding of it. In France, on the other hand, positivism's influence (and, to a lesser extent, that of its founder Comte) was only more gradually felt as it allied itself with the forces of social change and the shifting tides of anti–Catholicism among the educated elites, which in turn gave positivism a more political and sociological than philosophical importance. Similar adaptations to local conditions occurred elsewhere. For a full discussion of these developments, see W. M. Simon, *European Positivism in the Nineteenth Century* (Ithaca, NY: Cornell University Press, 1963). Simon's book, regrettably, is really

a history of Comtean positivism rather than positivism per se, and thus his net is not as widely cast into the waters of nineteenth century thought (especially philosophical developments in Germany) as one might wish.

[8]Pannekoek follows both Lenin and Engels in his selection of Moleschott, Vogt, and Büchner as representative of nineteenth century materialism. Haeckel's main works post–dated Engels' career. For a complete discussion of the movement, including its forebears, see Frederick Gregory, *Scientific Materialism in Nineteenth Century Germany* (Boston: D. Reidel, 1977)

[9]Moleschott's *Der Krieslauf des Lebens* (Mainz: V. von Zabern, 1852) went through numerous editions before the end of the century. In an notable exception to these men's general independence from their immediate philosophical predecessors, the materialist Feuerbach's Heidelberg lectures of 1848 did influence the scientific research of Jacob Moleschott. Moleschott's groundbreaking work on nutrition and the importance of trace elements in foodstuffs for proper growth and development, which he called "medical materialism," was considered revolutionary at the time, especially by Feuerbach. See Eugene Kamenka, *The Philosophy of Ludwig Feuerbach* (New York: Praeger, 1970), 30.

[10]Karl Vogt, *Köhlerglaube und Wissenschaft* [Blind Faith and Science], 2nd ed. (Giessen: J. Ricker, 1855), 32.

[11]His *Kraft und Stoff*, a classic statement of this renewed materialism, went through twelve editions within the first seventeen years after its appearance in 1855.

[12]For a fuller discussion of the impact of Darwinism upon the whole of German intellectual life after 1859, see Richard Weikart, *Socialist Darwinism: Evolution in German Socialist Thought from Marx to Bernstein* (San Francisco: International Scholars Publications, 1999).

[13]Haeckel's fierce opposition to all forms of religion (despite his continued membership in the Evangelical Church until 1903), his fervent support for the application of scientific methodology to the analysis of contemporary social and political questions, and his opposition to "the utter nonsense of socialist leveling" extended his popularity far beyond narrow philosophical circles and made him one of the most important social theorists of the Second Reich. In fact, his mixture of biology and politics later earned him the admiration of the Nazis, who frequently invoked his writings in defense of their racial policies.

[14]For a more extended and sympathetic discussion of Haeckel's thought, see David H. Degrood, *Haeckel's Theory of the Unity of Nature: A Monograph in the History of Philosophy* (Amsterdam: B. R. Gruner, 1982).

[15]Ibid., 88.

[16]Ernst Mach, *Principles of the Theory of Heat: Historically and Critically Elucidated*, ed. Brian McGuinness (Dordrecht: B. Reidel, 1986).

[17]Leszek Kolakowski, *Main Currents of Marxism, in 3 vols.: vol. 2: The Golden Age*, tr. P. S. Falla (Oxford: Oxford University Press, 1978), 428. For consistency, I have conformed (by the use of brackets) Kolakowski's translation of Avenarius' technical terminology to that of Pannekoek.

[18] Staurt MacIntyre summarizes nicely when he writes: "Dietzgen's early writings earned qualified public praise from Marx, who presented him to the Hague Conference as 'our philosopher'; and from Engels, who in *Ludwig Feuerbach and the Outcome of Classical German Philosophy* credited him with the independent discovery of the materialist dialectic. In private correspondence Marx and Engels

were more patronising about his deficiencies of formal education" (see "Josef Dietzgen," in *A Dictionary of Marxist Thought* [op. cit.]). Pannekoek, writing as he did without access to a complete edition of Marx and Engel's correspondence, can be excused for not knowing this.

[19]V.I. Lenin, *Collected Works*, 45 vols (Moscow: Progress Publishers, 1960-70; hereafter *CW*).

[20]John Gerber, "The Formation of Pannekoek's Marxism," in Serge Bricianer, ed., *Pannekoek and the Workers' Councils* (St. Louis: Telos, 1978), 1–30, 5.

[21]Ibid., 4.

[22]Ibid., 4.

[23]Ibid., 4, 6.

[24]Joseph Dietzgen, *The Positive Outcome of Philosophy*, tr. Ernest Untermann, with an introduction by Dr. Anton Pannekoek (Chicago: Charles H. Kerr and Co., 1906). The best discussion of Pannekoek's relationship to and dependence upon Dietzgen is that of Gerber, "The Formation of Pannekoek's Marxism," pp. 3–8.

[25]Dietzgen is not indexed in any of the volumes, nor can I find him mentioned even in such likely discussions as that of Lenin's *Materialism and Empirio–criticism*. While Lenin gives some favorable mention to Dietzgen in *Materialism and Empirio–Criticism* (*CW* 14:117–22, 243–50) this is practically the last mention he receives from any philosopher of consequence.

[26]Robert C. Williams, *The Other Bolsheviks: Lenin and His Critics, 1904–1914* (Bloomington: Indiana University Press, 1986).

[27]Kolakowski, *Main Currents*, 2:420.

[28]A. Bogdanov, *Empiriomonizm*, 3 vols. (Moscow, 1904–1907).

[29]David G. Rowley, "Bogdanov and Lenin: Epistemology and Revolution," in *Studies in East European Thought* 48 (1996): 1–19. I am indebted to Rowley's excellent article for many of the details of my discussion of Bogdanov.

[30]Ibid., 5.

[31]Ibid., 5.

[32]Neil Harding, *Lenin's Political Thought, vol. 1: Theory and Practice in the Democratic Revolution* (New York: Macmillan, 1979), 279.

[33]Rowley, "Bogdanov and Lenin," 6.

[34]*CW* 14:229: "A philosophy that teaches that physical nature itself is a product, is a philosophy of clericalism pure and simple.... If nature is a product, it is obvious it can be a product only of something that is greater, richer, broader, mightier than nature, of something that exists; for in order to 'produce' nature, it must exist independently of nature. That means that something exists *outside* nature, something which moreover *produces* nature. In plain language this is called God."

[35]Harding, *Lenin's Political Thought*, 1:281.

[36]Rowley, "Bogdanov and Lenin," 12.

[37]*CW* 14:123.

[38]*CW* 14:358.

[39]Louis Althusser, "Lenin and Philosophy," in *Lenin and Philosophy and other essays*, tr. Ben Brewster (New York: Monthly Review, 1971), 49.

[40]There are several excellent biographical essays on various aspects of Pannekoek's work. His philosophical development is detailed by John Gerber, "The Formation of Pannekoek's Marxism," in Serge Bricianer, ed., *Pannekoek and the Workers' Councils* (op. cit.), 1–30; for a discussion of his scientific work, see

Bricianer's "Author's Introduction," *ibid.*, 31–56. Pannekoek's political activity is discussed at length the introduction to D. A. Smart, ed., *Pannekoek and Gorter's Marxism* (London: Pluto Press, 1978), 7–49; see also John Gerber, "From Left Radicalism to Council Communism: Anton Pannekoek and German Revolutionary Marxism," in *Journal of Contemporary History* 23:2 (1988), 169–189. Each of these writers, it should be noted, were by virtue of their interest in Council communism far more sympathetic to Pannekoek's philosophical efforts than the present author.

[41]One of the worst decisions by Pannekoek was to ignore the Machist controversy in his attack on Lenin, limiting himself instead to a discussion of Mach's philosophy. This complete silence on the influence of Mach within Marxism, especially Russian Marxism, during the first decade of the century is inexcusable, since even Lenin—hardly a model of scholarly balance—offered at least a caricature of this "Machism" in his own work. In Pannekoek's defense, this silence is probably due more to an inability to read the Russian sources as it was to any particular malice or bias on his part. But especially in a work devoted to attacking Lenin's philosophy, such an omission is unforgivable since without some knowledge of the influence of Mach's thought on Russian Marxism, Lenin's decision to attack it in *Materialism and Empirio–criticism* is unintelligible.

[42]Z. A. Jordan, *The Evolution of Dialectical Materialism*, 121, citing R. von Mises, *Positivism: A Study in Human Understanding*, trans. J. Bernstein and R. G. Newton (New York: Goerge Braziller, 1956), 205. Both men, I believe, underestimate the influence of positivism in the social sciences of Germany in this period. More recently, there has been a greater appreciation of the influence of positivism on social and historical studies (or at least of their methodlogical commonalities). See, for instance, Eckhardt Fuchs, *Henry Thomas Buckle: Geschichtschreibung und Positivismus in England und Deutschland* (Leipzig: Leipziger Universitätsverlag, 1994). In any case, the physical sciences assimilated positivism quickly, especially its empiricist epistemology. For a solid (if somewhat popular) discussion, see J. B. Stallo, *The Concepts and Theories of Modern Physics* (Cambridge, Mass.; Harvard University Press, 1960).

[43]Serge Bricianer's claim that "this Dutchman was one of the few Marxists to attempt a real assessment of contemporary scientific ideology" ("Introduction," in *Pannekoek and the Workers' Councils* [*op. cit.*], 31–55, 36]) is actually quite misleading. Pannekoek was much less critical of scientific methodology and ideology than his contemporary Georg Lukacs, in comparison with whom he fares extremely poorly.

[44]This quotation, from Pannekoek's unpublished manuscript "Herrineringen uit de arbeidersbewegung", is translated and cited by Bricianer, "Pannekoek and the Workers' Councils," 5.

[45]See below, p. 87.

[46]See below, p. 101.

[47]See below, p. 87.

[48]Gerber, "Formation," 10–11.

[49]When Pannekoek does give a passing reference to this matter (see below, pp. 119-120), his views are remarkably similar to those of Bogdanov, if much less developed. John Gerber (ibid., 18) does attempt to draw some parallels between Pannekoek's Marxism and the classical Western Marxist critiques of modern

science as an ideological rather than an "objective" discipline. Martin Jay briefly acknowledges this effort without passing judgment upon it. See his excellent *Marxism and Totality: The Adventures of a Concept from Lukacs to Habermas* (Berkeley: University of California Press, 1984), 7, n.10. However, Pannekoek is only a "Western Marxist" by virtue of his geographical (Germany, the Netherlands, and, ultimately, the United States) and his political (Council Communist and Anti–Leninist) locations. Philosophically, little or no evidence exists to place him in this category.

[50]See below, p. 107.

[51]See below, p. 109.

[52]See below, p. 106.

[53]See below, p. 110-111.

[54]See below, p. 110.

[55]This passage is quoted from Bricianer, "Author's Introduction," 50. Bricianer here is condensing Pannekoek's essay "Society and Mind in Marxian Philosophy," *Science and Society* 1:4 (1937).

[56]See below, p. 74.

[57]See below, p. 69.

[58]Karl Marx and Frederick Engels, *Collected Works*, 50 vols. (New York: International Publishers, 1975–) 3: 345–46. Admittedly, the question of the ontological implications of Marx's early writings on human praxis are much more complex than presented here, and whether they lead inevitably to a Lukacsian version of Hegelianism is among the more important debates within the Marxist tradition. For a fuller discussion of this question, see Martin Jay, *Marxism and Totality: The Adventures of a Concept from Lukacs to Habermas* (op. cit.); Gavin Kitching, *Karl Marx and the Philosophy of Praxis* (London: Routledge, 1988); and Carol C. Gould, *Marx's Social Ontology: Individuality and Community in Marx's Theory of Social Reality* (Cambridge, Mass.: MIT Press, 1981). A more orthodox but less illuminating response to Western Marxist developments of this topic can be found in John Hoffman, *Marxism and the Theory of Praxis: A Critique of Some New Versions of Old Fallacies* (New York: International Publishers, 1976). Regardless of the outcome of this debate, though, the inadequacy, indeed, the simplicity, of Pannekoek's formulation and its conceptual distance from Marx's writings is obvious.

[59]Gerber, "Formation," 12.

[60]The size of the bibliography of Lenin studies is simply staggering. Even the writings on him in English prior to 1980 fill an entire volume of almost five hundred pages (David R. Egan and Melinda Egan, eds., *V. I. Lenin: An Annotated Bibliography of English Sources until 1980* [Lanham, Maryland: Scarecrow Press, 1982]), with similar amounts of material available in the major European languages. The size of the Russian material produced during the Soviet years, while perhaps inversely proportional to its scholarly value, is even larger.

[61]*CW* 14:29.

[62]*CW* 14:51.

[63]*CW* 14:232.

[64]*CW* 14:51.

[65]*CW* 14:69.

[66]*CW* 14:41.

[67] *CW* 14:69: "The 'naive realism' of any healthy person who has not been an inmate of a lunatic asylum or a pupil of idealist philosophers consists in the view that things, the environment, the world, exist *independently* of our sensation, of our consciousness, of our *self* and of man in general."

[68] One of the very few exceptions is Bakhurst, *Consciousness and Revolution* (op. cit.), which not only takes Lenin seriously as a philosopher but also attempts to salvage from the Soviet literature those critics and commentators who moved beyond "angelology" or "demonology" in their interpretation of his thought.

[69] Among these few exceptions, G. A. Paul's "Lenin's Theory of Perception" (op. cit.) stands as one of the finest examples.

[70] *CW* 14:159.

[71] *CW* 14:361.

[72] *CW* 14:235.

[73] *CW* 14:256–257.

[74] *CW* 14:175–176.

[75] *CW* 14:190.

[76] *CW* 14:104–105.

[77] *CW* 14:110.

[78] Bakhurst, *Consciousness and Revolution*, 120.

[79] Ruben, *Marxism and Materialism*, chap. 6, esp. 185–189.

[80] *CW* 14:69–70.

[81] *CW* 14:265.

[82] *CW* 14:55.

[83] Even there, though, his progress amounts to little more than a recognition of these problems while thinking through Hegelian and Kantian criticisms of traditional materialism. See, for example, Anderson, *Lenin, Hegel, and Western Marxism*, 75–76.

[84] *CW* 14:26.

[85] *CW* 14:60.

[86] Gustav A. Wetter, *Dialectical Materialism: A Historical and Systematic Survey or Philosophy in the Soviet Union*, tr. Peter Heath (New York: Frederick A. Praeger, 1960), 117.

[87] *CW* 14:258.

[88] *CW* 14:96.

[89] *CW* 14:129.

[90] *CW* 14:130.

[91] *CW* 14:260–261.

[92] Paul, "Lenin's Theory of Perception," 73.

Note on the Text

*L*enin als Philosoph was originally published in Amsterdam in mimeograph form in 1938 under the pseudonym J. Harper. The author's English translation was first published in 1948 and reissued unchanged by Merlin Press in 1975 (with accompanying essays by Paul Mattick and Karl Korsch). From an editorial and stylistic perspective, there is no satisfactory edition of this text. Pannekoek's translation suffers from his lack of fluency in English, while the text appears to have had almost no stylistic or scholarly controls placed on it prior to publication. Therefore, following the most recent edition of the German text [*Lenin als Philosoph,* Hrsg. von Alfred Schmidt (Frankfurt am Main: Europäische Verlagsanstalt Frankfurt, 1969)], minor editorial changes have been made throughout the text (e.g., the correction of obvious misspellings and typographical errors); various names have been brought into conformity with contemporary American spelling and usage (e.g., Bolshevist has been changed to Bolshevik, Plechanov to Plekhanov, etc.); and Pannekoek's punctuation has been corrected when necessary to clarify his meaning (e.g., the replacement of double quotation marks with single ones when used for emphasis rather than direct quotation).

L. B. Richey

Introduction

The Russian Revolution was fought under the banner of Marxism. In the years of propaganda before the First World War the Bolshevik Party came forward as the champion of Marxist ideas and tactics. It worked along with the radical tendencies in the socialist parties of Western Europe, which were also steeped in Marxian theory, whereas the Menshevik Party corresponded rather to the reformist tendencies over here.[1] In theoretical controversies the Bolshevik authors, besides the so–called Austrian and Dutch schools of Marxism, came forward as the defenders of rigid Marxist doctrines.[2] In the Revolution the Bolsheviks, who now had adopted the name of Communist Party, could win because they put up as the leading principle of their fight the class war of the working masses against the bourgeoisie. Thus Lenin and his party, in theory and practice, stood as the foremost representatives of Marxism.

Then, however, a contradiction appeared. In Russia a system of state–capitalism consolidated itself, not by deviating from but by following Lenin's ideas (e.g., in his *State and Revolution*).[3] A new dominating and exploiting class came into power over the working class. But at the same time Marxism was fostered, and proclaimed the fundamental basis of the Russian state. In Moscow a "Marx–Engels Institute" was founded that collected with care and reverence all the well–nigh lost and forgotten works and manuscripts of the masters and published them in excellent editions. Whereas the Communist Parties, directed by the Moscow Comintern, refer to Marxism as their guiding doctrine, they meet with more and more opposition from the most advanced workers in Western Europe and America, most radically from the ranks of Council communism.[4] These contradictions, extending over all important problems of life and of the social struggle, can be cleared up only by penetrating into the deepest, i.e., the philosophical principles of what is called Marxism in these different trends of thought.

Lenin gave an exposition of his philosophical ideas in his work *Materialism and Empirio–criticism* that appeared in Russian in 1908, and was published in 1927 in German and in English translations.[5] Some of the Russian socialist intellectuals about 1904 had taken an interest in modern Western natural philosophy, especially in the ideas of Ernst Mach, and tried to combine these with Marxism.[6] A kind of *Machism*, with Bogdanov, Lenin's most intimate collaborator, and Lunacharsky as spokesmen, developed as an influential trend in the socialist party.[7] After the first revolution the strife flared up again, connected as it was with all the various tactical and practical differences in the socialist movement. Then Lenin took a decisive stand against these deviations and, aided by Plekhanov, the ablest representative of Marxian theory among the Russians, soon succeeded in destroying the influence of Machism in the socialist party.[8]

In the Introduction to the German and English editions of Lenin's book, Deborin—at that time the official interpreter of Leninism, but afterwards disgraced—exalts the importance of the collaboration of the two foremost theoretical leaders for the definite victory of true Marxism over all anti–marxist, reformist trends.

> Lenin's book is not only an important contribution to philosophy, but it is also a remarkable document of an intra–party struggle which was of utmost importance in strengthening the general philosophical foundations of Marxism and Leninism, and which to a great degree determined the subsequent growth of philosophical thought amongst the Russian Marxists.... Unfortunately, matters are different beyond the borders of the Soviet Union, . . . where Kantian scholasticism and positivistic idealism are in full bloom.[9]

Since the importance of Lenin's book is so strongly emphasized here, it is necessary to make it the subject of a serious critical study. The doctrine of Party Communism of the Third International cannot be judged adequately unless their philosophical basis is thoroughly examined.

Marx's studies on society, which for a century now have been dominating and shaping the workers' movement in increased measure, took their form from German philosophy. They cannot be understood without a study of the spiritual and political developments of the European world. Thus it is with other social and philosophical trends and with other schools of materialism developing besides Marxism. Thus it is, too, with the theoretical ideas underlying the Russian revolution. Only by comparing these different systems of thought as to their social origin and their philosophical contents can we arrive at a well–founded judgment.

Marxism

The evolution of Marx's ideas into what is now called Marxism can be understood only in connection with the social and political developments of the period in which they arose. It was the time when industrial capitalism made its entry into Germany. This brought about a growing opposition to the existing aristocratic absolutism. The ascending bourgeois class needed freedom of trade and commerce, favorable legislation, a government sympathetic to its interests, freedom of press and assembly, in order to secure its needs and desires in an unhampered fight. Instead it found itself confronted with a hostile regime, an omnipotent police, and a press censorship which suppressed every criticism of the reactionary government. The struggle between these forces, which led to the revolution of 1848, first had to be conducted on a theoretical level, as a struggle of ideas and a criticism of the prevailing system of ideas. The criticism of the young bourgeois intelligentsia was directed mainly against religion and Hegelian philosophy.

Hegelian philosophy, in which the self–development of the 'Absolute Idea' creates the world and then, as developing world, enters the consciousness of man, was the philosophical guise suited to the Christian world of the epoch of the 'Restoration' after 1815. Religion handed down by past generations served, as always, as the theoretical basis and justification for the perpetuation of old class relations. Since an open political fight was still impossible, the struggle against the feudal oligarchy had to be conducted in a veiled form, as an attack on religion. This was the task of the group of young intellectuals of 1840 among whom Marx grew up and rose to a leading position.[10]

While still a student Marx admitted, although reluctantly, the force of the Hegelian method of thought, dialectics, and made it his own. That he chose for his doctor's thesis the comparison of the two great materialistic philosophers of ancient Greece, Democritus and Epicurus, seems to indicate, however, that in the deep recesses of subconsciousness Marx inclined to materialism.[11] Shortly thereafter he was called upon to assume the editorship of a new paper founded by the oppositional Rheinish bourgeoisie in Cologne. Here he was drawn into the practical problems of the political and social struggle. So well did he conduct the fight that after a year of publication the paper was banned by the State authorities. It was during this period that Feuerbach made his final step towards materialism. Feuerbach brushed away Hegel's fantastic system, turned towards the simple experiences of everyday life, and arrived at the conclusion that religion was a man–made product.[12] Forty years later Engels still spoke fervently of the liberating effect that Feuerbach's work had on his contemporaries, and of the enthusiasm it aroused in Marx, despite critical reservations.[13] To Marx it meant that now instead of attacking a heavenly image they had to come to grips with earthly realities. Thus in 1843 in his essay *Kritik der Hegelschen Rechtsphilosophie* (A Criticism of the Hegelian Philosophy of Law) he wrote:

> As far as Germany is concerned the criticism of religion is practically completed; and the criticism of religion is the basis of all criticism . . . . The struggle against religion is indirectly the struggle against that world whose spiritual aroma is religion . . . . Religion is the moan of the oppressed creature, the sentiment of a heartless world, as it is the spirit of spiritless conditions. It is the opium of the people. The abolition of religion as the illusory happiness of the people is the demand for their real happiness, the demand to abandon the illusions about their condition is a demand to abandon a condition which requires illusions. The criticism of religion therefore contains potentially the criticism of the Vale of Tears whose aureole is religion. Criticism has plucked the imaginary flowers which adorned the chain, not that man should wear his fetters denuded of fanciful embellishment, but that he should throw off the chain and break the living flower . . . . Thus the criticism of heaven is transformed into the criticism of earth, the criticism of religion into the criticism of Law and the criticism of theology into the criticism of politics.[14]

The task confronting Marx was to investigate the realities of social life. In collaboration with Engels during their stay in Paris and Brussels, he made a study of the French Revolution and French socialism, as well as of English economy and the English working–class movement, which led towards further elaboration of the doctrine known as 'Historical Materialism.' As the theory of social development by way of class struggles we find it expounded in *La misère de la philosophie* (written in 1846 against Proudhon's *Philosophie de la misère*), in the *Communist Manifesto* (1848), and in the oft–quoted Preface to *Zur Kritik der Politischen Oekonomie* (1859).[15]Marx and Engels themselves refer to this system of thought as materialism, in opposition to the 'idealism' of Hegel and the Young Hegelians. What do they understand by materialism? Engels, discussing afterwards the fundamental theoretical problems of Historical Materialism in his *Anti–Dühring* and in his booklet on Feuerbach, states in the latter publication:

> The great basic question of all philosophy, especially of modern philosophy, is that concerning the relation of thinking and being . . . . Those who asserted the primacy of the spirit to nature and, therefore, in the last instance, assumed world–creation in some form or other, comprised the camp of idealism. The others, who regarded nature as primary, belong to the various schools of materialism.[16]

That not only the human mind is bound up with the material organ of the brain, but that, also, man with his brain and mind is intimately connected with the rest of the animal kingdom and the inorganic world, was a self–evident truth to Marx and Engels. This conception is common to all "schools of materialism." What distinguishes Marxist materialism from other schools must be learned from its various polemic works dealing with practical questions of politics and society. Then we find that to Marx materialistic thought was a working method. It was meant to explain all phenomena by means of the material world, the existing realities. In his writings he does not deal with philosophy, nor does he formulate materialism in a system of philosophy; he is utilizing it as a method for the study of the world, and thus demonstrates its validity. In the essay quoted above, for example, Marx does not demolish the Hegelian philosophy of law by philosophical disputations, but through an annihilating criticism of the real conditions in Germany.

In the materialist method philosophical sophistry and disputations around abstract concepts are replaced by the study of the real world. Let us take a few examples to elucidate this point. The statement 'Man proposes, God disposes' is interpreted by the theologian from the point of view of the omnipotence of God. The materialist searches for the cause of the discrepancy between expectations and results, and finds it in the social effects of commodity exchange and competition. The politician debates the desirability of freedom and of socialism; the materialist asks: from what individuals or classes do these demands spring, what specific content do they have, and to what social need do they correspond? The philosopher, in abstract speculations about the essence of time, seeks to establish whether or not absolute time exists. The materialist compares clocks to see whether simultaneousness or succession of two phenomena can be established unmistakably.

Feuerbach had preceded Marx in using the materialist method, insofar as he pointed out that religious concepts and ideas are derived from material conditions. He saw in living man the source of all religious thoughts and concepts. *Der Mensch ist was er ißt* (Man is what he eats) is a well–known German pun summarizing his doctrine. Whether his materialism would be valid, however, depended on whether he would be successful in presenting a clear and convincing explanation of religion. A materialism that leaves the problem obscure is insufficient and will fall back into idealism. Marx pointed out that the mere principle of taking living man as the starting point is not enough. In his Theses on Feuerbach in 1845 he formulated the essential difference between his materialistic method and Feuerbach's as follows:

> Feuerbach resolves the religious essence into the human essence (*das menschliche Wesen*). But the human essence is no abstraction inherent in each single individual. In its reality it is the ensemble of the social relationships. (Thesis 6) His work consists in the dissolution of the religious world into its secular basis. The fact,

however, that the secular foundation lifts itself above itself and establishes itself in the clouds as an independent realm is only to be explained by the self–cleavage and self–contradictions of this secular basis. The latter itself, therefore, must first be understood in its contradictions, and then, by the removal of the contradiction, must be revolutionized in practice. (Thesis 4)[17]

In short, man can be understood only as a social being. From the individual we must proceed to society, and then the social contradictions out of which religion came forth, must be dissolved. The real world, the material, sensual world, where all ideology and consciousness have their origin, is the developing human society—with nature in the background, of course, as the basis on which society rests and of which it is a part transformed by man.

A presentation of these ideas may be found in the manuscript of *Die Deutsche Ideologie* (The German Ideology), written in 1845 but not published.[18] The part that deals with Feuerbach was first published in 1925 by Ryazanov, then chief of the Marx–Engels Institute in Moscow; the complete work was not published until 1932.[19] Here the theses on Feuerbach are worked out at greater length. Although it is manifest that Marx wrote it down quite hurriedly, he nevertheless gave a brilliant presentation of all the essential ideas concerning the evolution of society, which later found their short expression, practically, in the proletarian propaganda pamphlet the *Communist Manifesto* and, theoretically, in the preface to *Zur Kritik der Politischen Oekonomie* (Critique of Political Economy).

The German Ideology is directed first of all against the dominant theoretical view which regarded consciousness as the creator, and ideas developing from ideas as the determining factors of human history. They are treated here contemptuously as "the phantoms formed in the human brain" that are "necessary sublimates of their material, empirically verifiable life process bound to material premises."[20] It was essential to put emphasis on the real world, the material and empirically given world as the source of all ideology. But it was also necessary to criticize the materialist theories that culminated in Feuerbach. As a protest against ideology, the return to biological man and his principal needs is correct; but it is not possible to find a solution to the question of how and why religious ideas originate if we take the individual as an abstract isolated being. Human society in its historical evolution is the dominant reality controlling human life. Only out of society can the spiritual life of man be explained. Feuerbach, in his attempt to find an explanation of religion by a return to the 'real' man did not find the real man, because he searches for him in the individual, the human being generally. From his approach the world of ideas cannot be explained. Thus he was forced to fall back on the ideology of universal human love. "Insofar as Feuerbach is a materialist," Marx said, "he does not deal with history, and insofar as he considers history, he is not a materialist."[21]

What Feuerbach could not accomplish was accomplished by the Historical Materialism of Marx: an explanation of man's ideas out of the material world. A brilliant survey of the historical development of society finds its philosophical summary in the sentence: "Men, developing their material production and their material intercourse, along with this, their real existence, alter their thinking and the products of their thinking."[22] Thus, as relation between reality and thinking, materialism is in practice proven to be right. We know reality only through the medium of the senses. Philosophy, as theory of knowledge, then finds its basis in this principle: the material, empirically given world is the reality which determines thought.

The basic problem in the theory of knowledge (epistemology) was always: what truth can be attributed to thinking. The term 'criticism of knowledge' (*Erkenntniskritik*) used by professional philosophers for this theory of knowledge, already implies a viewpoint of doubt.[23] In his second and fifth theses on Feuerbach Marx refers to this problem and again points to the practical activity of man as the essential content of his life:

> The question whether objective truth can be attributed to human thinking is not a question of theory but a *practical* question. In practice man must prove the truth, i.e., the reality and power, the this–sidedness of his thinking. (Thesis 2) Feuerbach, not satisfied with *abstract* thinking, appeals to sensuous perception (*Anschauung*), but he does not conceive sensuousness (*die Sinnlichkeit*) as a *practical* human–sensuous activity. (Thesis 5)[24]

Why practical? Because man in the first place must live. His bodily structure, his faculties and his abilities, and all his activity are adapted to this very end. With these he must assert himself in the external world, i.e., in nature, and as an individual in society. To these abilities belongs the activity of the organ of thought, the brain, and the faculty of thinking itself. Thinking is a bodily faculty. In every phase of life man uses his power of thought to draw conclusions from his experiences, on which expectations and hopes are built, and these conclusions regulate his behavior and his actions. The correctness of his conclusions, the truth of his thinking, is shown by the very fact of his existence, since it is a condition for his survival. Because thinking is an efficient adaptation to life, it embodies truth, not for every conclusion, but in its general character. On the basis of his experiences man derives generalizations and rules, natural laws, on which his expectations are based. They are generally correct, as is witnessed by his survival. Sometimes, however, false conclusions may be drawn, with failure and destruction in their wake. Life is a continuous process of learning, adaptation, development. Practice is the unsparing test of the correctness of thinking.

Let us first consider this in relation to natural science. In the practice of this science, thought finds its purest and most abstract form. This is why philosophical scientists take this form as the subject of their deductions and pay little attention to its similarity to the thinking of everybody in his everyday activity. Yet thinking in the study of nature is only a highly developed special field in the entire social labor process. This labor process demands an accurate knowledge of natural phenomena and its integration into 'laws of nature', in order to utilize them successfully in the field of technics. The determination of these laws through observation of special phenomena is the task of specialists. In the study of nature it is generally accepted that practice, experiment, is the test of truth. Here, too, we find that the observed regularities, formulated as laws of nature, are generally fairly dependable guides to human practice; though they are frequently not entirely correct and often balk expectation, they are improved constantly through the progress of science. If, therefore, man at times was referred to as the 'legislator of nature' it must be added that nature often disregards his laws and summons him to make better ones.

The practice of life, however, comprises much more than the scientific study of nature. The relation of the scientist to the world, despite his experiments, remains observational. To him the world is an external thing to look at. But in reality man deals with nature in his practical life by acting upon it and making it part of his existence. Man does not stand against nature as to an external alien world. By the toil of his hands man transforms the world, to such an extent that the original natural substance is hardly discernible, and in this process transforms himself too. Thus man himself builds his new world: human society, imbedded in nature transformed into a technical apparatus. Man is the creator of this world. What meaning, then, has the question of whether his thinking embodies truth? The object of his thinking is what he himself produces by his physical and mental activities, and which he controls through his brain.

This is not a question of partial truths. Engels in his booklet on Feuerbach referred to the synthesizing of the natural dye alizarin (contained in madder) as a proof of the truth of human thinking.[25] This, however, proves only the validity of the chemical formula employed; it cannot prove the validity of materialism as against Kant's 'Thing–in–itself.' This concept, as may be seen from Kant's preface to his *Critique of Pure Reason*, results from the incapacity of bourgeois philosophy to understand the earthly origin of moral law. The 'Thing–in–itself' is not refuted by chemical industry but by Historical Materialism explaining moral law through society. It was Historical Materialism that enabled Engels to see the fallacy of Kant's philosophy, to prove the fallaciousness for which he then offered other arguments.[26] Thus, to repeat, it is not a question of partial truths in a specific field of knowledge, where the practical outcome affirms or refutes them. The point in question is a philosophical one, namely, whether human thought is capable of grasping the deepest truth of the world. That the philosopher in his secluded study, who handles exclusively abstract philosophical concepts, which are derived in turn from abstract scientific concepts themselves formulated outside of practical life—that he, in the midst of this world of shadows, should have his doubts, is easily understood. But for human beings, who live and act in the practical everyday world, the question cannot have any meaning. The truth of thought, says Marx, is nothing but the power and mastery over the real world.

Of course this statement implies its counterpart: thinking cannot embody truth where the human mind does not master the world. When the products of man's hand—as Marx expounded in *Das Kapital*—grow into a power over him, which he no longer controls and which in the form of commodity–exchange and capital confronts him as an independent social being, mastering man and even threatening to destroy him, then his mind submits to the mysticism of supernatural beings and he doubts the ability of his thinking to distinguish truth.[27] Thus in the course of past centuries the myth of supernatural heavenly truth unknowable to man overshadowed the materialistic practice of daily experiences. Not until society has evolved to a state where man will be able to comprehend all social forces and will have learned to master them—in communist society, in short—will his thinking entirely correspond to the world. But already before, when the nature of social production as a fundamental basis of life and future development has become clear to man, when the mind—be it only theoretically at first—actually masters the world, our thinking will be fully true. That means that by the science of society as formulated by Marx, because now his thesis is fulfilled, materialism gains permanent mastery and becomes the only conformable philosophy. Thus Marxian theory of society in principle means a transformation of philosophy.

Marx, however, was not concerned with pure philosophy. "Philosophers have interpreted the world differently, but what matters is to change it," he says in his last thesis on Feuerbach.[28] The world situation pressed for practical action. At first inspired by the rising bourgeois opposition to absolutism, then strengthened by the new forces that emanated from the struggle of the English and French working class against the bourgeoisie, Marx and Engels, through their study of social realities, arrived at the conclusion that the proletarian revolution following on the heels of the bourgeois revolution would bring the final liberation of mankind. From now onward their activity was devoted to this revolution, and in the *Communist Manifesto* they laid down the first directions for the workers' class struggle.

Marxism has since been inseparably connected with the class fight of the proletariat. If we ask what Marxism is, we must first of all understand that it does not encompass everything Marx ever thought and wrote. The views of his earlier years, for instance, such as quoted above, are representative only in part; they are phases in a development leading toward Marxism. Neither was it complete at once; whereas the role of the proletarian class struggle and the aim of communism is already outlined in the *Communist Manifesto*, the theory of capitalism and surplus value is developed much later. Moreover, Marx's ideas themselves developed with the change of social and political conditions. The character of the revolution and the part played by the State in 1848, when the proletariat had only begun to appear, differed in aspect from that of later years at the end of the century, or today. Essential, however, are Marx's new contributions to science. There is first of all the doctrine of Historical Materialism, the theory of the determination of all political and ideological phenomena, of spiritual life in general, by the productive forces and relations. The system of production, itself based on the state of productive forces, determines the development of society, especially through the force of the class struggle. There is, furthermore, the presentation of capitalism as a temporary historical phenomenon, the analysis of its structure by the theory of value and surplus value, and the explanation of its revolutionary tendencies through the proletarian revolution towards communism. With these theories Marx has enriched human knowledge permanently. They constitute the solid foundation of Marxism as a system of thought. From them further conclusions may be drawn under new and changed circumstances.

Because of this scientific basis, however, Marxism is more than a mere science. It is a new way of looking at the past and the future, at the meaning of life, of the world, of thought; it is a spiritual revolution, it is a new world–view, a new life–system. As a system of life Marxism is real and living only through the class that adheres to it. The workers who are imbued with this new outlook, become aware of themselves as the class of the future, growing in number and strength and consciousness, striving to take production into their own hands, and through the revolution to become masters of their own fate. Hence Marxism as the theory of proletarian revolution is a reality, and at the same time a living power, only in the minds and hearts of the revolutionary working class.

Thus Marxism is not an inflexible doctrine or a sterile dogma of imposed truths. Society changes, the proletariat grows, science develops. New forms and phenomena arise in capitalism, in politics, in science, which Marx and Engels could not have foreseen or surmised. Forms of thought and struggle that under former conditions were necessary must under later conditions give way to other ones. But the method of research which they framed remains up to this day an excellent guide and tool towards the understanding and interpretation of new events. The working class, enormously increased under capitalism, today stands only at the threshold of its revolution and, hence, of its Marxist development; Marxism only now begins to get its full significance as a living force in the working class. Thus Marxism itself is a living theory which grows with the increase of the proletariat and with the tasks and aims of its fight.

Middle–Class Materialism

Returning now to the political scene out of which Marxism emerged, it must be noted that the German revolution of 1848 did not bring full political power to the bourgeoisie. But after 1850 capitalism developed strongly in France and Germany. In Prussia the Progressive Party began its fight for parliamentarism, whose inner weakness became evident later when the government through military actions met the demands of the bourgeoisie for a strong national State. Movements for national unity dominated the political scene of Central Europe. Everywhere, with the exception of England where it already held power, the rising bourgeoisie struggled against the feudal absolutist conditions.

The struggle of a new class for power in State and society is at the same time always a spiritual struggle for a new world view. The old powers can be defeated only when the masses rise up against them or, at least, do not follow them any longer. Therefore it was necessary for the bourgeoisie to make the working masses its followers and win their adherence to capitalist society. For this purpose the old ideas of the petty bourgeoisie and the peasants had to be destroyed and supplanted with new bourgeois ideologies. Capitalism itself furnished the means to this end.

The natural sciences are the spiritual basis of capitalism. On the development of these sciences depends the technical progress that drives capitalism forward. Science, therefore, was held in high esteem by the rising bourgeois class. At the same time this science freed them from the conventional dogmas embodying the rule of feudalism. A new outlook on life and on the world sprang up out of the scientific discoveries, and supplied the bourgeoisie with the necessary arguments to defy the pretensions of the old powers. This new world outlook it disseminated among the masses. To the peasant farm and the artisan workshop belongs the inherited biblical faith. But as soon as the sons of the peasants or the impoverished artisans become industrial workers their mind is captured by capitalist development. Even those who remain in pre–capitalistic conditions are lured by the more liberal outlook of capitalist progress and become susceptible to the propaganda of new ideas.

The spiritual fight was primarily a struggle against religion. The religious creed is the ideology of past conditions; it is the inherited tradition which keeps the masses in submission to the old powers and which had to be defeated. The struggle against religion was imposed by the conditions of society; hence it had to take on varying forms with varying conditions. In those countries where the bourgeoisie had already attained full power, as for instance in England, the struggle was no longer necessary and the bourgeoisie paid homage to the established church. Only among the lower middle class and among the workers did more radical trends of thought find some adherence. In countries where industry and the bourgeoisie had to fight for emancipation they proclaimed a liberal, ethical Christianity in opposition to the orthodox faith. And where the struggle against a still powerful royal and aristocratic class was difficult, and required the utmost strength and exertion, the new world view had to assume extreme forms of radicalism and gave rise to middle–class materialism. This was so to a great extent in Central Europe; so it is natural that most of the popular propaganda for materialism (Moleschott, Vogt, Büchner) originated here, though it found an echo in other countries.[29] In addition to these radical pamphlets, a rich literature popularizing the modern scientific discoveries appeared, supplying valuable weapons in the struggle to free the masses of the citizens, the workers, and the peasants, from the spiritual fetters of tradition, and to turn them into followers of the progressive bourgeoisie. The middle–class intelligentsia—professors, engineers, doctors—were the most zealous propagandists of the new Enlightenment.

The essence of natural science was the discovery of laws operating in nature. A careful study of natural phenomena disclosed recurring regularities which allowed for scientific predictions. The seventeenth century had already known the Galilean law of falling bodies and gravity, Kepler's laws of the planetary motions, Snell's law of the refraction of light, and Boyle's law of the gas pressure. Towards the end of the century came the discovery of the law of gravitation by Newton, which more than all preceding discoveries exerted a tremendous influence in the philosophical thought of the eighteenth and nineteenth centuries. Whereas the others were rules that were not absolutely correct, Newton's law of gravitation proved to be the first real exact law strictly dominating the motions of the heavenly bodies, which made possible predictions of the phenomena with the same precision with which they could be observed. From this the conception developed that all natural phenomena follow entirely rigid definite laws. In nature causality rules: gravity is the cause of bodies falling, gravitation causes the movements of the planets. All occurring phenomena are effects totally determined by their causes, allowing for neither free will, nor chance nor caprice.

This fixed order of nature disclosed by science was in direct contrast to the traditional religious doctrines in which God as a despotic sovereign arbitrarily rules the world and deals out fortune and misfortune as he sees fit, strikes his enemies with thunderbolts and pestilence and rewards others with miracles. Miracles are contradictory to the fixed order of nature; miracles are impossible, and all reports about them in the Bible are fables. The biblical and religious interpretations of nature belong to an epoch in which primitive agriculture prevailed under the overlordship of absolute despots. The natural philosophy of the rising bourgeoisie, with its natural laws controlling all phenomena, belongs to a new order of state and society where the arbitrary rule of the despot is replaced by laws valid for all.

The natural philosophy of the Bible, which theology asserts to be absolute, divine, truth is the natural philosophy of ignorance that has been deceived by outward appearances, that saw an immovable earth as the center of the universe, and held that all matter was created and was perishable. Scientific experience showed, on the contrary, that matter which apparently disappeared (as for instance in burning) actually changes into invisible gaseous forms. Scales demonstrated that a reduction of the total weight did not occur in this process and that, therefore, no matter disappeared. This discovery was generalized into a new principle: matter cannot be destroyed, its quantity always remains constant, only its forms and combinations change. This holds good for each chemical element; its atoms constitute the building stones of all bodies. Thus science with its theory of the conservation of matter, of the eternity of nature, opposed the theological dogma of the creation of the world some six thousand years ago.

Matter is not the only persistent substance science discovered in the transient phenomena. Since the middle of the nineteenth century the law known as the conservation of energy came to be regarded as the fundamental axiom of physics. Here, too, a fixed and far reaching order of nature was observed; in all phenomena changes of the form of energy take place: heat and motion, tension and attraction, electrical and chemical energy; but the total quantity never changes. This principle led to an understanding of the development of cosmic bodies, the sun and the earth, in the light of which all the assertions of theology appeared like the talk of a stuttering child.

Of even greater consequence were the scientific discoveries concerning man's place in the world. Darwin's theory of the origin of species, which showed the evolution of man from the animal kingdom, was in complete contradiction to all religious doctrines. But even before Darwin, discoveries in biology and chemistry revealed the organic identity of all human and living creatures with non–organic nature. The protoplasm, the albuminous substance of which the cells of all living beings are composed and to which all life is bound, consists of the same atoms as all other matter. The human mind, which was elevated into a part of divinity by the theological doctrine of the immortal soul, is closely bound up with the physical properties of the brain; all spiritual phenomena are the accompaniment to or the effect of material occurrences in the brain cells.

Middle–class materialism drew the most radical conclusions from these scientific discoveries. Everything spiritual is merely the product of material processes; ideas are the secretion of the brain, just as bile is the secretion of the liver. Let religion—said Büchner—go on talking about the fugacity of matter and the immortality of the mind; in reality it is the other way around. With the least injury of the brain everything spiritual disappears; nothing at all remains of the mind when the brain is destroyed, whereas the matter, its carrier, is eternal and indestructible. All phenomena of life, including human ideas, have their origin in the chemical and physical processes of the cellular substance; they differ from non–living matter only in their greater complexity. Ultimately all their processes must be explained by the dynamics and movements of the atoms.

These conclusions of natural–science materialism, however, could not be upheld to their utmost consequences. After all, ideas are different from bile and similar bodily secretions; mind cannot be considered as a form of force or energy, and belongs in a quite different category. If mind is a product of the brain which differs from other tissues and cells only in degree of complexity, then, fundamentally, it must be concluded that something of mind, some sensation, is to be found in every animal cell. And because the cellular substance is only an aggregate of atoms, more complex but in substance not different from other matter, the conclusion must be that something of what we call mind is already present in the atom: in every smallest particle of matter there must be a particle of the 'spiritual substance.' This theory of the 'atom–soul' we find in the works of the prominent zoologist Ernst Haeckel, energetic propagandist of Darwinism and courageous combatter of religious dogmatism.[30] Haeckel did not consider his philosophical views as materialism but called them monism—strangely enough since he extends the duality of mind–matter down to the smallest elements of the world.

Materialism could dominate the ideology of the bourgeois class only for a short time. Only so long as the bourgeoisie could believe that its society of private property, personal liberty, and free competition, through the development of industry, science and technique, could solve the life problems of all mankind—only so long could the bourgeoisie assume that the theoretical problems could be solved by science, without the need to assume supernatural and spiritual powers. As soon, however, as it became evident that capitalism could not solve the life problems of the masses, as was shown by the rise of the proletarian class struggle, the confident materialist philosophy disappeared. The world was seen again full of insoluble contradictions and uncertainties, full of sinister forces threatening civilization. So the bourgeoisie turned to various kinds of religious creeds, and the bourgeois intellectuals and scientists submitted to the influence of mystical tendencies. Before long they were quick to discover the weaknesses and shortcomings of materialist philosophy, and to make speeches on the 'limitations of science' and the insoluble 'world–riddles.'

Only a small number of the more radical members of the lower and middle classes, who clung to the old political slogans of early capitalism, continued to hold materialism in respect. Among the working class it found a fertile ground. The adherents of anarchism always were its most convinced followers. Socialist workers embraced the social doctrines of Marx and the materialism of natural science with equal interest. The practice of labor under capitalism, their daily experience and their awakening understanding of social forces contributed greatly towards undermining traditional religion. Then, to solve their doubts, the need for scientific knowledge grew, and the workers became the most zealous readers of the works of Büchner and Haeckel. Whilst Marxist doctrine determined the practical, political and social ideology of the workers, a deeper understanding asserted itself only gradually; few became aware of the fact that middle–class materialism had long since been outdated and surpassed by Historical Materialism. This, by the way, concurs with the fact that the working–class movement had not yet reached beyond capitalism, that in practice the class struggle only tended to secure its place within capitalist society, and that the democratic solutions of the early middle–class movements were accepted as valid for the working class also. The full comprehension of revolutionary Marxist theory is possible only in connection with revolutionary practice.

Wherein, then, do middle–class materialism and Historical Materialism stand opposed to one another?

Both agree insofar as they are materialist philosophies, that is, both recognize the primacy of the experienced material world; both recognize that spiritual phenomena, sensation, consciousness, ideas, are derived from the former. They are opposite in that middle–class materialism bases itself upon natural science, whereas Historical Materialism is primarily the science of society. Bourgeois scientists observe man only as an object of nature, the highest of the animals, determined by natural laws. For an explanation of man's life and action, they have only general biological laws and, in a wider sense, the laws of chemistry, physics, and mechanics. With these means little can be accomplished in the way of understanding social phenomena and ideas. Historical Materialism, on the other hand, lays bare the specific evolutionary laws of human society and shows the interconnection between ideas and society.

The axiom of materialism that the spiritual is determined by the material world, has therefore entirely different meanings for the two doctrines. For middle–class materialism it means that ideas are products of the brain, are to be explained out of the structure and the changes of the brain substance, finally out of the dynamics of the atoms of the brain. For Historical Materialism, it means that the ideas of man are determined by his social conditions; society is his environment which acts upon him through his sense organs. This postulates an entirely different kind of problem, a different approach, a different line of thought, hence, also a different theory of knowledge.[31]

For middle–class materialism the problem of the meaning of knowledge is a question of the relationship of spiritual phenomena to the physico–chemical–biological phenomena of the brain matter. For Historical Materialism it is a question of the relationship of our thoughts to the phenomena which we experience as the external world. Now man's position in society is not simply that of an observing being; he is a dynamic force which reacts upon his environment and changes it. Society is nature transformed through labor. To the scientist, nature is the objectively given reality which he observes, which acts on him through the medium of his senses. To him the external world is the active and dynamic element, whilst the mind is the receptive element. Thus it is emphasized that the mind is only a reflection, an image of the external world, as Engels expressed it when he pointed out the contradiction between the materialist and idealist philosophies. But the science of the scientist is only part of the whole of human activity, only a means to a greater end. It is the preceding, passive part of his activity which is followed by the active part: the technical elaboration, the production, the transformation of the world by man.

Man is in the first place an active being. In the labor process he utilizes his organs and aptitudes in order to constantly build and remake his environment. In this procedure he not only invented the artificial organs we call tools, but also trained his physical and mental aptitudes so that they might react effectively to his natural environment as instruments in the preservation of life. His main organ is the brain whose function, thinking, is as good a physical activity as any other. The most important product of brain activity, of the efficient action of the mind upon the world, is science, which stands as a mental tool next to the material tools and, itself a productive power, constitutes the basis of technology and so an essential part of the productive apparatus.

Hence Historical Materialism looks upon the works of science, the concepts, substances, natural laws, and forces, although formed out of the stuff of nature, primarily as the creations of the mental labor of man. Middle–class materialism, on the other hand, from the point of view of the scientific investigator, sees all this as an element of nature itself which has been discovered and brought to light by science. Natural scientists consider the immutable substances, matter, energy, electricity, gravity, the law of entropy, etc., as the basic elements of the world, as the reality that has to be discovered. From the viewpoint of Historical Materialism they are products which creative mental activity forms out of the substance of natural phenomena.

This is one fundamental difference in the method of thinking. Another difference lies in dialectics which Historical Materialism inherited from Hegel. Engels has pointed out that the materialist philosophy of the eighteenth century disregarded evolution; it is evolution that makes dialectic thinking indispensable. Evolution and dialectics since have often been regarded as synonymous; and the dialectical character of Historical Materialism is supposed to be rendered by saying that it is the theory of evolution. Evolution, however, was well known in the natural science of the nineteenth century. Scientists were well acquainted with the growth of the cell into a complex organism, with the evolution of animal species as expressed in Darwinism, and with the theory of evolution of the physical world known as the law of entropy. Yet their method of reasoning was undialectical. They believed the concepts they handled to be fixed objects, and considered their identities and opposites as absolutes. So the evolution of the world as well as the progress of science brought out contradictions, of which many examples have been quoted by

Engels in his *Anti–Dühring*. Understanding in general and science in particular segregate and systematize into fixed concepts and rigid laws what in the real world of phenomena occurs in all degrees of flux and transition. Because language separates and defines groups of phenomena by means of names, all items falling into a group, as specimens of the concept, are considered similar and unchangeable. As abstract concepts, they differ sharply, whereas in reality they transform and merge into one another. The colors blue and green are distinct from each other but in the intermediary nuances no one can say where one color ends and the other begins. It cannot be stated at what point during its life–cycle a flower begins or ceases to be a flower. That in practical life good and evil are not absolute opposites is acknowledged everyday, just as that extreme justice may become extreme injustice. Juridical freedom in capitalist development manifests itself as actual slavery. Dialectical thinking is adequate to reality in that in handling the concepts it is aware that the finite cannot fully render the infinite, nor the static the dynamic, and that every concept has to develop into new concepts, even into its opposite. Metaphysical, undialectical thinking, on the other hand, leads to dogmatic assertions and contradictions because it views conceptions formulated by thought as fixed, independent entities that make up the reality of the world.

Natural science proper, surely, does not suffer much from this shortcoming. It surmounts difficulties and contradictions in practice insofar as continually it revises its formulations, increases their richness by going into finer details, improves the qualitative distinctions by mathematical formulas, completes them by additions and corrections, thereby bringing the picture ever closer to the original, the world of phenomena. The lack of dialectical reasoning becomes disturbing only when the scientist passes from his special field of knowledge towards general philosophical reasonings, as is the case with middle–class materialism.

Thus, for instance, the theory of the origin of species often leads to the notion that the human mind, having evolved from the animal mind, is qualitatively identical with the latter and has only increased in quantity. On the other hand, the qualitative difference between the human and the animal mind, a fact of common experience, was raised by theological doctrine, in enunciating the immortality of the soul, into an absolute antithesis. In both cases there is a lack of dialectical thinking according to which a similarity in original character, when through the process of growth the increasing quantitative difference turns into qualitative difference—the so–called inversion of quantity into quality—requires new names and characteristics, without leading to complete antithesis and loss of affinity.

It is the same metaphysical, non–dialectical thinking to compare thought, because it is the product of brain processes with such products of other organs as bile; or to assume that mind, because it is a quality of some material substance, must be a characteristic quality of all matter. And especially, to think that because mind is something other than matter, it must belong to an absolutely and totally different world without any transition, so that a dualism of mind and matter, reaching down to the atoms, remains sharp and unbridgeable. To dialectical thinking mind simply is a concept incorporating all those phenomena we call spiritual, which, thus, cannot reach beyond their actual appearance in the lowest living animals. There the term mind becomes questionable, because the spiritual phenomena disappear gradually into mere sensibility, into the more simple forms of life. 'Mind' as a characteristic existing quality, a separate something, which either is or is not there, does not exist in nature; mind is just a name we attach to a number of definite phenomena, some perceived clearly, others uncertainly, as spiritual.

Life itself offers a close analogy. Proceeding from the smallest microscopic organisms to still smaller invisible bacteria and viruses, we finally come to highly complicated albuminous molecules that fall within the sphere of chemistry. Where in this succession living matter ceases to exist and dead matter begins cannot be determined; phenomena change gradually, become simplified, are still analogous and yet already different. This does not mean that *we* are unable to ascertain demarcation lines; it is simply the fact that nature knows of no boundaries. A condition or quality 'life', which either is or is not present, does not exist in nature; again life is a mere name, a concept we form in order to comprehend the endless variety of gradations in life phenomena. Because middle–class materialism deals with life and death, matter and mind, as if they were genuine realities existing in themselves, it is compelled to work with hard and sharp opposites, whereas nature offers an immense variety of more or less gradual transitions.

Thus the difference between middle–class materialism and Historical Materialism reaches down to basic philosophical views. The former, in contradiction to the comprehensive and perfectly realistic Historical Materialism, is illusory and imperfect—just as the bourgeois class movement, of which it was the theory, represented an imperfect and illusory emancipation, in contrast to the complete and real emancipation by way of the proletarian class struggle.

The difference between the two systems of thought shows itself practically in their position towards religion. Middle–class materialism intended to overcome religion. However, a certain view arisen out of social life cannot be vanquished and destroyed merely by refuting it with argumentation; this means posing one point of view against another; and every argument finds a counter–argument. Only when it is shown why, and under what circumstances such a view was necessary, can it be defeated by establishing the transient character of these conditions. Thus the disproof of religion by natural science was effective only insofar as the primitive religious beliefs were concerned, where ignorance about natural laws, about thunder and lightning, about matter and energy, led to all kinds of superstition. The theory of bourgeois society was able to destroy the ideologies of primitive agricultural economy. But religion in bourgeois society is anchored in its unknown and uncontrollable social forces; middle–class materialism was unable to deal with them. Only the theory of the workers' revolution can destroy the ideologies of bourgeois economy. Historical Materialism explains the social basis of religion and shows why for certain times and classes it was a necessary way of thought. Only thus was its spell broken. Historical Materialism does not fight religion directly; from its higher vantage point it understands and explains religion as a natural phenomenon under definite conditions. But through this very insight it undermines religion and foresees that with the rise of a new society religion will disappear. In the same way Historical Materialism is able to explain the temporary appearance of materialist thought among the bourgeoisie, as well as the relapse of this class into mysticism and religious trends. In the same way, too, it explains the growth of materialist thought among the working class as being not due to any antireligious argument but to the growing recognition of the real forces in capitalist society.

Dietzgen

Middle–class materialism, when it came up in Western Europe in connection with the fight of the middle class for emancipation, was inevitable in practice; but as theory it was a retrogression compared with Historical Materialism. Marx and Engels were so far ahead that they saw it only as a backsliding into obsolete ideas of the eighteenth century Enlightenment. Because they saw so very clearly the weaknesses of the bourgeois political fight in Germany—while underrating the vitality of the capitalist system—they did not give much attention to the accompanying theory. Only occasionally they directed at it some contemptuous words, to refute any identification of the two kinds of materialism. During their entire lifetime their attention was concentrated upon the antithesis of their theory to the idealist systems of German philosophy, especially Hegel. Middle–class materialism, however, was somewhat more than a mere repetition of eighteenth century ideas; the enormous progress of the science of nature in the nineteenth century was its basis and was a source of vigor. A criticism of its foundations had to tackle problems quite different from those of post–Hegelian philosophy. What was needed was a critical examination of the fundamental ideas and axioms which were universally accepted as the results of natural science and which were in part accepted by Marx and Engels too.

Here lies the importance of the writings of Joseph Dietzgen.[32] Dietzgen, an artisan, a tanner living in Rhineland, who afterwards went to America and there took some part in the working class movement, was a self–made socialist philosopher and author. In social and economic matters he considered himself a pupil of Marx, whose theory of value and capital he entirely comprehended. In philosophy he was an independent, original thinker, who set forth the philosophical consequences of the new world view. Marx and Engels, though they honorably mentioned him as "the philosopher of the proletariat," did not agree with everything he wrote; they blamed his repetitions, often judged him confused, and it is doubtful whether they ever understood the essence of his arguments, far removed from their own mode of thinking.[33] Indeed, whereas Marx expresses the new truth of his views as precise statements and sharp logical arguments, Dietzgen sees his chief aim in stimulating his readers to think for themselves on the problem of thinking. For this purpose he repeats his arguments in many forms, exposes the reverse of what he stated before, and assigns to every truth the limits of its truth, fearing above all that the reader should accept any statement as a dogma. Thus he teaches practical dialectics. Whereas in his later writings he is often vague, his first work "The nature of human brain work" (1869), and his later "A socialist's excursions into the field of epistemology" (1877), as well as some smaller pamphlets, are brilliant contributions to the theory of knowledge.[34] They form an essential part in the entirety of the world view that we denote by the name of Marxism. The first problem in the science of human knowledge, the origin of ideas, was answered by Marx in the demonstration that they are produced by the surrounding world. The second, adjoining problem, how the impressions of the surrounding world are transformed into ideas, was answered by Dietzgen. Marx stated what realities determine thought; Dietzgen established the relation between reality and thought. Or, in the words of Herman Gorter, "Marx pointed out what the world does to the mind, Dietzgen pointed out what the mind does itself."[35]

Dietzgen proceeds from the experiences of daily life, and especially from the practice of natural science. "Systematization is the essence, is the general expression of all activity of science. Science seeks only by our understanding to bring the objects of the world into order and system."[36] Human mind takes from a group of phenomena what is common to them (e.g., from a rose, a cherry, a setting sun their color), leaves out their specific differences, and fixes their general character (red) in a concept; or it expresses as a rule what repeats itself (e.g., stones fall to the earth). The object is concrete, the spiritual concept is abstract. "By means of our thinking we have, potentially, the world twofold, outside as reality, inside, in our head, as thoughts, as ideas, as an image. Our brains do not grasp the things themselves but only their concept, their general image. The endless variety of things, the infinite wealth of their characters, finds no room in our mind."[37] For our practical life indeed, in order to foresee events and make predictions, we do not want all the special cases but only the general rule. The antithesis of mind and matter, of thought and reality, of spiritual and material, is the antithesis of abstract and concrete, of general and special.

This, however, is not an absolute antithesis. The entire world, the spiritual as well as the visible and tangible world, is object to our thinking. Things spiritual do exist, they too are really existing, as thoughts; thus they too are materials for our brain activity of forming concepts. The spiritual phenomena are assembled in the concept of mind. The spiritual and the material phenomena, mind and matter together, constitute the entire real world, a coherent entity in which matter determines mind and mind, through human activity, determines matter. That we call this total world a unity means that each part exists only as a part of the whole, is entirely determined by the action of the whole, that, hence, its qualities and its special character consists in its relations to the rest of the world. Thus also mind, i.e., all things spiritual, is a part of the world's totality, and its nature consists in the totality of its relations to the world's whole, which we then, as the object of thinking, oppose to it under the name material, outer, or real world. If now we call this material world primary and the mind dependent, it means for Dietzgen simply that the entirety is primary and the part secondary. Such a doctrine where spiritual and material things, entirely interdependent, form one united world, may rightly be called monism.

This distinction between the real world of phenomena and the spiritual world of concepts produced by our thinking is especially suitable to clear up the nature of scientific conceptions. Physics has discovered that the phenomena of light can be explained by rapid vibrations propagated through space, or, as the physicists said, through space–filling ether. Dietzgen quotes a physicist stating that these waves are the real nature of light whereas all that we see as light and color is only an appearance. "The superstition of philosophical speculation here," Dietzgen remarks, "has led us astray from the path of scientific induction, in that waves rushing through the ether with a velocity of 40,000 (German) miles per second, and constituting the true nature of light are opposed to the real phenomena of light and color. The perversion becomes manifest where the visible world is denoted as a product of the human mind, and the ether vibrations, disclosed by the intellect of the most acute thinkers, as the corporeal reality."[38] It is quite the reverse, Dietzgen says: the colored world of phenomena is the real world, and the ether waves are the picture constructed by the human mind out of these phenomena.

It is clear that in this antagonism we have to do with different meanings about the terms truth and reality. The only test to decide whether our thoughts are truth is always found in experiment, practice, experience. The most direct of experiences is experience itself; the experienced world of phenomena is the surest of all things, the most indubitable reality. Surely we know phenomena that are only appearances. This means that the evidences of different senses are not in accordance and have to be fitted in a different way in order to get a harmonious world–picture. Should we assume the image behind the mirror, which we can see but cannot touch, as a common reality, then such a confused knowledge would bring practical failure. The idea that the entire world of phenomena should be nothing but appearance could make sense only if we assumed another source of knowledge—e.g., a divine voice speaking in us—to be brought in harmony with the other experiences.

Applying now the same test of practice to the physicist we see that his thinking is correct also. By means of his vibrating ether he not only explained known phenomena but even predicted in the right way a number of unsuspected new phenomena. So his theory is a good, a true theory. It is truth because it expresses what is common to all these experiences in a short formula that allows of easy deduction of their endless diversity. Thus the ether waves must be considered a true picture of reality. The ether itself of course cannot be observed in any way; observation shows only phenomena of light.

How is it then, that the physicists spoke of the ether and its vibrations as a reality? Firstly as a model, conceived by analogy. From experience we know of waves in water and in the air. If now we assume such waves in another, finer substance filling the universe, we may transfer to it a number of well–known wave–phenomena, and we find these confirmed. So we find our world of reality growing wider. With our spiritual eyes we see new substances, new particles moving, invisible because they are beyond the power of our best microscopes, but conceivable after the model of our visible coarser substances and particles.

In this way, however, with ether as a new invisible reality, the physicists landed into difficulties. The analogy was not perfect; the world–filling ether had to be assigned qualities entirely different from water or air; though called a substance it deviated so completely from all known substances that an English physicist once compared it somehow to pitch. When it was discovered that light waves were electromagnetic vibrations, it ensued that the ether had to transmit electric and magnetic phenomena too. For this role, a complicated structure had to be devised, a system of moving, straining, and spinning contrivances, that might be used as a coarse model, but which nobody would call the true reality of this finest of fluids filling space between the atoms. The thing became worse when in the beginning of the twentieth century the theory of relativity came up and denied the existence of ether altogether. Physicists then grew accustomed to deal with a void space, equipped however with qualities expressed in mathematical formulas and equations. With the formulas the phenomena could be computed in the right way; the mathematical symbols were the only thing remaining. The models and images were nonessential, and the truth of a theory does not mean anything more than that the formulas are exact.

Things became worse still when phenomena were discovered that could be represented only by light consisting of a stream of so–called quanta, separated particles hurrying through space. At the same time the theory of vibrations held the field too, so that according to needs one theory or the other had to be applied. Thus two strictly contradictory theories both were true, each to be used within its group of phenomena. Now at last physicists began to suspect that their physical entities, formerly considered the reality behind the phenomena, were only images, abstract concepts, models more easily to comprehend the phenomena. When Dietzgen half a century before wrote

his views which were simply a consequence of Historical Materialism, there was no physicist who did not firmly believe in the reality
of world–ether. The voice of a socialist artisan did not penetrate in
the university lecture rooms. Nowadays it is precisely the physicists
who assert that they are dealing with models and images only, who
are continually discussing the philosophical basis of their science,
and who emphasize that science aims solely at relations and formulas
through which future phenomena may be predicted from former ones.

In the word phenomenon, 'that which appears', there is contained
an oppositeness to the reality of things; if we speak of 'appearings'
there must be something else that appears. Not at all, says Dietzgen;
phenomena appear (or occur), that is all. In this play of words we
must not think, of course, of what appears to me or to another ob-
server; all that happens, whether man sees it or not, is a phenomenon, and all these happenings form the totality of the world, the
real world of phenomena. "Sense perception shows an endless transformation of matter . . . . The sensual world, the universe at any place
and any time is a new thing that did not exist before. It arises and
passes away, passes and arises under our hands. Nothing remains the
same, lasting is only perpetual change, and even the change varies . .
. . The (middle–class) materialist, surely, asserts the permanency, eternity, indestructibility of matter . . . . Where do we find such eternal,
imperishable, formless matter? In the real world of phenomena we
meet only with forms of perishable matter . . . . Eternal and imperishable matter exists practically, in reality, only as the sum total of its
perishable phenomena."[39] In short, matter is an abstraction.

Whereas philosophers spoke of the essence of things, physicists
spoke of matter, the lasting background behind the changing phenomena. Reality, they say, is matter; the world is the totality of matter. This matter consists of atoms, the invariable ultimate building
stones of the universe, that by their various combinations impose the
impression of endless change. On the model of surrounding hard
objects, as an extension of the visible world of stones, grains, and
dust, these still smaller particles were assumed to be the constituents
of the entire world, of the fluid water as well as of the formless air.
The truth of the atomic theory has stood the test of a century of
experience, in an endless number of good explanations and success-

ful predictions. Atoms of course are not observed phenomena themselves; they are inferences of our thinking. As such they share the
nature of all products of our thinking; their sharp limitation and
distinction, their precise equality belongs to their abstract character.
As abstractions they express what is general and common in the phenomena, what is necessary for predictions.

To the physicist, of course, atoms were no abstractions but real
small invisible particles, sharply limited, exactly alike for every chemical element, with precise qualities and precise mass. But modern science destroyed also this illusion. Atoms, firstly, have been dissolved
into still smaller particles, electrons, protons, neutrons, forming complicated systems, some of them inaccessible to any experiment, mere
products of the application of logic. And these smallest elements of
the world cannot be considered as precisely defined particles finding
themselves at definite points in space. Modern physical theory assigns to each of them the character of a wave motion extending over
infinite space. When you ask the physicist what it is that moves in
such waves his answer consists in pointing to a mathematical equation. The waves are no waves of matter, of course; that which moves
cannot even be called a substance, but is rendered most truly by the
concept of probability; the electrons are probability–waves. Formerly
a particle of matter in its invariable weight presented a precisely defined quantity, its mass. Now mass changes with the state of motion
and cannot be separated accurately from energy; energy and mass
change into one another. Whereas formerly these concepts were neatly
separated and the physical world was a clear system without contradiction, proudly proclaimed the real world, physics nowadays, when
it assumes its fundamental concepts matter, mass, energy as fixed,
well separated entities, is plunged into a crowd of unsolvable contradictions. The contradiction is cleared up when we simply consider
them as what they are: abstractions serviceable to render the ever
extending world of phenomena.

The same holds for the forces and laws of nature. Here Dietzgen's
expositions are not adequate and somewhat confused, probably because at the time the German physicists used the word *Kraft* indis-
criminately for force and for energy. A simple practical case such as
gravity may easily clear up the matter. Gravity, physicists said, is the

cause of falling. Here cause is not something preceding the effects and different from it; cause and effect are simultaneous and express the same thing in different words. Gravity is a name that does not contain anything more than the phenomena themselves; in denoting them by this word we express the general, the common character of all the phenomena of falling bodies. More essential than the name is the law; in all free movements on earth there is a constant downward acceleration. Writing the law as a mathematical formula we are able to compute the motions of all falling or thrown bodies. It is not necessary now to keep the phenomena all in our head; to know future cases it is sufficient to know the law, the formula. The law is the abstract concept our mind constructed out of the phenomena. As a law it is a precise statement that is assumed to hold good absolutely and universally, whereas the phenomena are diversified and always show deviations which we then ascribe to other, accessory causes.

Newton extended the law of gravity to the celestial motions. The orbit of the moon was 'explained' by showing that it was pulled by the same force that made stones fall onto earth; so the unknown was reduced to the known. His law of universal gravitation is expressed by a mathematical formula through which astronomers are able to compute and predict the celestial phenomena; and the result of countless predictions shows the truth of the law. Scientists now called the gravitation the 'cause' of all these motions; they saw it as a reality floating in space, a kind of mysterious imp, a spiritual being called a 'force' directing the planets in their course; the law was a command somehow present in nature which the bodies had to obey. In reality there is nothing of the sort; 'cause' means the short summary or compendium, 'effect' means the diverse multitude of phenomena. The formula binding the acceleration of each particle to its distance from the other ones, expresses in a short form exactly the same course of things as does a lengthy description of the actual motions. Gravitation as a separate something pulling and steering the bodies does not exist in nature but only in our head. As a mysterious command permeating space it has no more real existence than has Snell's law of refraction as a command to the light rays on how they have to go. The course of the light rays is a direct mathematical consequence of the different velocity of light in different substances; instead of by the command of a law it can equally well be represented by the principle that light, as [if—Editor] it were an intelligent being, chooses the quickest route to reach the aim.[40] Modern science, in an analogous way, in the theory of relativity, renders the motions in space not by gravitational force, but by prescribing the shortest road (the 'geodesic') in the distorted four–dimensional space–time. Now again physicists came to consider this warped space as a 'reality' behind the phenomena. And again it must be stated that, like Newton's gravitation, it is only a mental abstraction, a set of formulas, better than the former, hence more true, because it represents more phenomena which the old law could not explain.

What is called 'causality' in nature, the reign of natural laws—sometimes one even speaks of the 'law of causality', i.e., in nature the law holds that laws hold—simply comes down to the fact that the regularities we find in the phenomena are expressed in the form of prescripts absolutely valid. If there are limitations, exceptions, conditions, they are expressly stated as such, and we try to represent them by correcting the law; this shows that its character is meant to be absolute. We are confident that it holds for future use; and if it fails, as often happens, or does not hold precisely, we represent this by additional 'causes.'

We often speak of the inexorable course of events, or of the necessity in nature; or we speak of 'determinism', as if this course had been determined and fixed by somebody in advance. All these human names chosen to express the antithesis to the arbitrariness and free choice in human actions, denoting a kind of compulsion, are a source of much confusion and cannot render exactly the character of nature. Rather we say that the entire nature at this moment depends entirely on what it was a moment before. Or perhaps better still: that nature in its totality and history is a unity, remaining identically itself in all its variations. All parts are interrelated as parts of one whole, and the laws of nature are the humanly imperfect expressions of these interrelations. Necessity can be ascribed to them solely in a partial imperfect degree; absolute necessity may be affirmed for the entirety of nature only. Phenomena may be imperfectly rendered by our laws; but we are convinced that they go on in a way which can be ultimately reduced to simple description, and could not be otherwise than they are.

The significance of Marxism is often expressed by saying that it presents, for the first time, a natural science of society. Hence society, just as nature, is determined by natural laws; society develops not by chance or incidentally but according to an overall necessity. And since society is human activity, then human action and choice and will are not arbitrary, not chance, but determined by social causes. What this means will now be clear. The totality of the world, consisting of nature and society, is a unity, at any moment determined by what it was before, each part entirely determined by the action of the rest. It remains the same identical world, in which the happenings of one part, of mankind or part of it, depend entirely on the surrounding world, nature and society together. Here too we try to find regularities, rules and laws, and we devise names and concepts; but seldom do we ascribe to them a separate reality. Whereas a physicist easily believes in gravitation as a real something floating in space around the sun and the planets, it is more difficult to believe in 'progress' or 'liberty' hovering round us and floating over society as real beings that conduct man like a ruling fate. They too are abstractions constructed by the mind out of partial relations and dependencies. With their 'necessity' it is as with all necessity in nature. Its basis is the necessity that man must eat to live. In this popular saying the fundamental connection of man with the entirety of the world is expressed.

Through the immense complication of social relations 'laws' of society are much more difficult to discern, and they cannot now be put into the form of exact formulas. Still more than in nature they may be said to express not the future but our expectation about the future. It is already a great thing that, whereas former thinkers were groping in the dark, now some main lines of development have been discovered. The importance of Marxism as a science of society is not so much the truth of the rules and expectations it formulated, but rather what is called its method: the fundamental conviction that everything in the world of mankind is directly connected with the rest. Hence for every social phenomenon we have to look for the material and social factors of reality on which it depends.

Mach

In the later part of the nineteenth century, middle–class society turned away more and more from materialism. The bourgeoisie, through the development of capitalism asserted its social mastery; but the rise of the working class movement proclaiming as its aim the annihilation of capitalism, led to misgivings as to the durability of the existing social system. World and future appeared full of unsolvable problems. Since the visible, material forces threatened mischief, the ruling class, to quiet its apprehensions and assure its self–reliance, turned to the belief in the superior rule of spiritual powers. Mysticism and religion gained the upper hand, and still more so in the twentieth century, after the First World War.

Natural scientists form a part of middle–class society; they are in continual contact with the bourgeoisie and are influenced by its spiritual trends. At the same time, through the progress of science, they have to deal with new problems and contradictions appearing in their concepts. It is not clear philosophical insight that inspires the criticism of their theories, but rather the immediate needs of their practical study of nature. This criticism then takes its form and color from the anti–materialist trends in the ruling class. Thus modern natural philosophy exhibits two characters: critical reflection over the principles of science, and a critical mood towards materialism. Just as in the time of Hegel, valuable progress in the theory of knowledge is garbed in mystical and idealistic forms.

Critics of the prevailing theories came forward, in the last part of the nineteenth century, in different countries: e.g., Karl Pearson in England, Gustav Kirchhoff and Ernst Mach in Germany, Henri Poincaré in France, all exhibiting, though in different ways, the same general trend of thought.[41] Among them the writings of Mach have doubtless exerted the greatest influence upon the ideas of the next generation.[42]

Physics, he says, should not proceed from matter, from the atoms, from the objects; these are all derived concepts. The only thing we know directly is experience, and all experience consists in sensations, sense impressions (*Empfindungen*). By means of our world of concepts, in consequence of education and intuitive custom, we express every sensation as the action of an object upon ourselves as subject: 'I see a stone.' But freeing ourselves from this custom we perceive that a sensation is a unit in itself, given directly without the distinction of subject and object. Through a number of similar sensations I come to the distinction of an object, and I know of myself too only by a totality of such sensations. Since object and subject are built up of sensations it is better not to use a name that points to a person experiencing them. So we prefer the neutral name of 'elements', as the simplest basis of all knowledge.

Ordinary thinking here finds the paradox that the hard immutable stone, the prototype of the solid 'thing' should be formed by, should 'consist of' such transient subjective stuff as sensations. On closer examination, however, we see that what constitutes the thing, its qualities, are simply this and nothing else. First its hardness is nothing but the totality of a number of often painful sensations; and secondly its immutability is the sum total of our experiences that on our returning to the same spot the same sensations repeat themselves. So we expect them as a fixed interconnection in our sensations. In our knowledge of the thing there is nothing that has not somehow the character of a sensation. The object is the sum total of all sensations at different times that, through a certain constancy of place and surroundings considered as related, are combined and denoted by a name. It is no more; there is no reason to assume with Kant a 'Thing–in–itself' (*Ding an sich*) beyond this sensation–mass; we cannot even express in words what we would have to think of it. So the object is formed entirely by sensations; it consists merely of sensations. Mach opposes his views to the current physical theory by the words:

> Not bodies produce sensations, but element–complexes (sensation–complexes) constitute the bodies. When the physicist consid-

ers the bodies as the permanent reality, the 'elements' as the transient appearance, he does not realize that all 'bodies' are only mental symbols for element–complexes (sensation–complexes).[43]

The same holds for the subject. What we denote by 'I myself' is a complex of recollections and feelings, former and present sensations and thoughts connected by continuity of memory, bound to a special body, but only partly permanent.

> What is primary is not myself but the elements . . . . The elements constitute the myself . . . . The elements of consciousness of one person are strongly connected, those of different persons are only weakly and passingly connected. Hence everybody thinks he knows only of himself as an indivisible and independent unity.[44]

In his work *Die Mechanik in ihrer Entwicklung* (The Development of Mechanics) he writes along the same lines:

> Nature consists of the elements given by the senses. Primitive man first takes out of them certain complexes of these elements that present themselves with a certain stability and are most important to him. The first and oldest words are names for 'things.' Here abstraction is made from the surroundings, from the continual small changes of these complexes, which are not heeded because they are not important. In nature there is no invariable thing. The thing is an abstraction, the name is a symbol for a complex of elements of which we neglect the changes. That we denote the entire complex by one word, one symbol, is done because we want to awaken at once all impressions that belong together . . . . The sensations are no 'symbols of things.' On the contrary the 'thing' is a mental symbol for a sensation–complex of relative stability. Not the things, the bodies, but colors, sounds, pressures, times (what we usually call sensations) are the true elements of the world. The entire process has an economical meaning. In picturing facts we begin with the ordinary more stable and habitual complexes, and afterwards for correction add what is unusual.[45]

In this treatment of the historical development of the science of mechanics he comes close to the method of Historical Materialism.

To him the history of science is not a sequence of geniuses producing marvelous discoveries. He shows how the practical problems are first solved by the mental methods of common life, until at last they acquire their most simple and adequate theoretical expression. Ever again the economic function of science is emphasized.

> The aim of all science is to substitute and to save experiences through the picturing and the forecastings of facts by thoughts, because these pictures are more easily at hand than the experiences themselves and in many respects may stand for them . . . . When we depict facts by thoughts we never imitate them exactly, but only figure those sides that are *important* for us; we have an aim that directly or indirectly arose out of practical interests. Our pictures are always abstractions. This again shows an economic trend.[46]

Here we see science, specialized as well as common knowledge, connected with the necessities of life, as an implement of existence.

> The biological task of science is to offer a most perfect orientation to man in the full possession of his senses.[47]

For man, in order to react efficiently to the impressions of his surroundings in each situation, it is not necessary to remember all former cases of analogous situations with their results. He has only to know what results generally, as a rule, and this determines his actions. The rule, the abstract concept is the instrument ready at hand that saves the mental consideration of all former cases. What natural law states is not what will happen and must happen in nature, but what we expect will happen; and that is the very purpose they have to serve.

The formation of abstract concepts, of rules and laws of nature, in common life as well as in science, is an intuitive process, intended to save brain work, aiming at economy of thinking. Mach shows in a number of examples in the history of science how every progress consists in greater economy, in that a larger field of experiences is compiled in a shorter way, so that in the predictions a repetition of the same brain operations is avoided. "With the short lifetime of man and his limited memory, notable knowledge is only attainable by the utmost economy of thinking." So the task of science consists in "representing facts as completely as possible by a minimum of brainwork."[48]

According to Mach the principle of economy of thinking determines the character of scientific investigation. What science states as properties of things and laws about atoms are in reality relations between sensations. The phenomena between which the law of gravitation establishes relations, consist in a number of visual, auditory or tactile impressions; the law says that they occur not by chance, and predicts how we may expect them. Of course we cannot express the law in this form; it would be inappropriate, unsuitable to practice because of its complexity. But as a principle, it is important to state that every law of nature deals with relations between phenomena. If now contradictions appear in our conceptions about atoms and world ether, they lie not in nature but in the forms we choose for our abstractions in order to have them available in the most tractable way. The contradiction disappears when we express the results of our research as relations between observed quantities, ultimately between sensations.

The unconcerned scientific view is easily obscured if a point of view fit for a limited aim is made the basis of all considerations. This is the case, says Mach, "when all experiences are considered as the effects of an outer world upon our consciousness. An apparently inextricable tangle of metaphysical difficulties results. The phantom disappears directly if we take matters in their mathematical form, and make it clear to ourselves that the establishment of functions and relations alone avails, and that the mutual dependence of experiences is the only thing we wish to know."[49] It might seem that Mach here expresses some doubts about the existence of an outer world independent of man. In countless other sentences, however, he speaks in a clear way of surrounding nature in which we have to live and which we have to investigate. It means that such an outer world as is accepted by physics and by ordinary opinion, the world of matter and forces as producing the phenomena, leads us into contradictions. The contradictions can be removed only if we return to the phenomena and instead of speaking words and abstract terms express our results as relations between observations. This is what was afterwards called Mach's principle: if we ask whether a statement has a meaning and what is its meaning, we have to look for what experiments may test it. It has shown its importance in modern times, first in discussions on time and space in the theory of relativity, and then in the understanding of atomic and radiation phenomena. Mach's aim was to find a broader field of interpretation for physical phenomena. In daily life the solid bodies are most adequate sensation–complexes, and mechanics, the science of their motions, was the first well–developed part of physics. But this reason does not justify our establishing the form and science of atoms as the pattern for the entire world. Instead of explaining heat, light, electricity, chemistry, biology, all in terms of such small particles, every realm should develop its own adequate concepts.

Yet there is a certain ambiguity in Mach's expressions on the outer world, revealing a manifest propensity towards subjectivism, corresponding to the general mystical trend in the capitalist world. Especially in later years he liked to discover cognate trends everywhere, and gave praise to idealistic philosophies that deny the reality of matter. Mach did not elaborate his views into a concise coherent system of philosophy with all consequences well developed. His aim was to give critical thoughts, to stimulate new ideas, often in paradoxes sharply pointed against prevailing opinions, without caring whether all his statements were mutually consistent and all problems solved. His was not a philosopher's mind constructing a system, but a scientist's mind, presenting his ideas as a partial contribution to the whole, feeling as part of a collectivity of investigators, sure that others will correct his errors and will complete what he left unachieved. "The supreme philosophy of a natural scientist," he says elsewhere, "is to be content with an incomplete world view and to prefer it to an apparently complete but unsatisfactory system."[50]

Mach's tendency to emphasize the subjective side of experience appears in that the immediately given elements of the world, which we call phenomena, are denoted as sensations. Surely this means at the same time a deeper analysis of the phenomena; in the phenomenon that a stone falls are contained a number of visual sensations combined with the memory of former visual and spatial sensations. Mach's elements, the sensations, may be called the simplest constituents of the phenomena. But when he says "Thus it is true that the world consists of our sensations" he means to point to the subjective character of the elements of the world.[51] He does not say 'my' sensations; solipsism (the doctrine that I myself only am existing) is entirely foreign to him and is expressly refuted; 'I myself' is itself a complex of sensations. But where he speaks of fellow–men in relation to the world of sensations, he is not entirely clear.

> Just as little as I consider red and green as belonging to an individual body, so little I make an essential difference—from this point of view of general orientation—between my sensations and another's sensations. The same elements are mutually connected in many 'myselfs' as their nodal points. These nodal points, however, are nothing perennial, they arise and disappear and change continually.[52]

Here it must be objected that "red" and "green" as belonging to more bodies are not the simple sensational elements of experience, but themselves already abstract concepts. It seems that Mach here replaces the abstract concepts body and matter by other abstract concepts, qualities and colors, that as realities appear in my and in another's sensations. And when he calls my sensation and another's analogous sensation the same element, this word is taken in another sense.

Mach's thesis that the world consists of our sensations expresses the truth that we know of the world only through our sensations; they are the materials out of which we build our world; in this sense the world, including myself, 'consists' of sensations only. At the same time, the emphasis upon the subjective character of sensations reveals the same middle–class trend of thought that we find in other contemporary philosophies. It is even more evident when he points out that these views may tend to overcome dualism, this eternal philosophical antithesis of the two worlds of matter and mind. The physical and the psychical world for Mach consist of the same elements, only in a different arrangement. The sensation green in seeing a leaf, with other sensations is an element of the material leaf; the same sensation, with others of my body, my eye, my reminiscences, is an element of 'myself', of my psyche.

Thus I see no antithesis of the physical and the psychical, but I see
a simple identity relative to these elements. In the sensual realm of
my consciousness every object is physical and psychical at the same
time . . . . Not the stuff is different in both realms, but the tendency
of the research.[53]

Thus dualism has disappeared; the entire world is a unity, consisting of the selfsame elements; and these elements are not atoms but
sensations. And in *Erkenntnis und Irrturm* he adds in a footnote:

There is no difficulty in building up every physical happening out
of sensations, i.e., psychical elements; but there is no possibility of
seeing how out of the usual physical elements, masses and motions,
any psychical happening might be constructed . . . . We have to
consider that nothing can be object of experience or science that
cannot be in some way a part of consciousness.[54]

Here, in this footnote added later, in 1905, the well–considered
equivalence of both worlds, physical and psychical, the careful neutral characterizing of the elements, is given up by calling them psychical, and the anti–materialistic spirit of the bourgeoisie breaks
through. Since it is not our aim to criticize and to contest but only to
set forth Mach's views we shall not enter into the tautology of the last
sentence, that only what is in consciousness can be conscious and
that hence the world is spiritual.

The new insight that the world is built up out of sensations as its
elements, meets with difficulties, Mach says, because in our uncritical youth we took over a world view that had grown intuitively in the
thousands of years of human development. We may break its spell by
critically repeating the process through conscious philosophic reasoning. Starting with the most simple experiences, the elementary
sensations, we construct the world step by step: ourselves, the outer
world, our body as part of the outer world, connected with our own
feelings, actions and reminiscences. Thus, by analogy, we recognize
fellow men as kindred, and so their sensations, disclosed by their
sayings, may be used as additional material in constructing the world.
Here Mach stops; further steps toward an objective world are not
made.

That this is no accidental incompleteness is shown by the fact that we find the same thing with Carnap, one of the leading thinkers in modern philosophy of science. In his work *Der logische Aufbau der Welt* (The Logical Construction of the World) he sets himself the same task, but more thoroughly: if we start with knowing nothing, having however our full capacity of thinking, how can we establish ('constitute') the world with all its contents?[55] I start with 'my sensations' and make them into a system of 'sayings' and 'objects' ('object' is the name given to everything about which we may utter a saying); thus I establish physical and psychical 'objects' and construct 'the world' as an ordered system of my sensations. The problem of dualism of body and mind, of material and spiritual, finds here the same answer as with Mach: both consist of the same materials, the sensations, only ordered in a different way. The sensations of fellow–men, according to their statements, lead to a physical world exactly corresponding to mine. So we call it the 'intersubjective world', common to all subjects; this is the world of natural science. Here Carnap stops, satisfied that dualism has been removed, and that any quest about the reality of the world is now shown to be meaningless, because 'reality' cannot be tested in another way than by our experience, our sensations. So the chain of progressive constitutings is broken off here.

It is easy to see the limitedness of this world structure. It is not finished. The world thus constituted by Mach and by Carnap is a momentary world supposed unchanging. The fact that the world is in continuous evolution is disregarded. So we must go on past where Carnap stopped. According to our experience people are born and die; their sensations arise and disappear, but the world remains. When my sensations out of which the world was constituted, cease with my death, the world continues to exist. From acknowledged scientific facts I know that long ago there was a world without man, without any living being. The facts of evolution, founded on our sensations condensed into science, establish a previous world without any sensations. Thus from an intersubjective world common to all mankind, constituted as a world of phenomena by science, we proceed to the constitution of an objective world. Then the entire world view changes. Once the objective world is constituted, all phenomena become independent of observing man, as relations between parts of the world. The world is the totality of an infinite number of parts acting upon another; every part consists in the totality of its actions and reactions with the rest, and all these mutual actions are the phenomena, the object of science. Man also is part of the world; we too are the totality of our mutual interactions with the rest, the outer world. Our sensations are now seen in a new light; they are the actions of the world upon us, only a small part of all happenings in the world, but, of course, the only ones immediately given to us. When now man is building up the world out of his sensations, it is a reconstruction in the mind of an already objectively existing world. Again we have the world twofold, with all the problems of epistemology, the theory of knowledge. How they may be solved without metaphysics is shown by Historical Materialism.

If one asks why two such prominent philosophers of science omitted this obvious step toward the constitution of an objective world, the answer can only be found in their middle–class world view. Their instinctive tenet is anti–materialistic. By adhering to the intersubjective world they have won a monistic world system, the physical world consisting of psychical elements, so that materialism is refuted. We have here an instructive example how class views determine science and philosophy.

Summarizing Mach's ideas we distinguish two steps. First the phenomena are reduced to sensations expressing their subjective character. Through the desire to find direct reality only in the sensations as psychical entities, he does not proceed by precise deductions to an objective world that obviously is matter of fact, though in a mystical, vague way. Then comes a second step from the world of phenomena to the physical world. What physics, and by the popular dispersion of science also common opinion, assumes as the reality of the world— matter, atoms, energy, natural laws, the forms of space and time, myself—are all abstractions from groups of phenomena. Mach combines both steps into one by saying that things are sensation–complexes.

The second step corresponds to Dietzgen; the similarity here is manifest. The differences are accounted for by their different class views. Dietzgen stood on the basis of dialectical materialism, and his expositions were a direct consequence of Marxism. Mach, borne by the incipient reaction of the bourgeoisie, saw his task in a fundamental criticism of physical materialism by asserting dominance to some spiritual principle. There is a difference, moreover, in personality and aims. Dietzgen was a comprehensive philosopher, eager to find out how our brains work; the practice of life and science was to him material for the knowledge of knowledge. Mach was a physicist who by his criticisms tries to improve the ways in which brains worked in scientific investigations. Dietzgen's aim was to give clear insight into the role of knowledge in social development, for the use of the proletarian struggle. Mach's aim was an amelioration of the practice of physical research, for the use of natural science.

Speaking of practice, Mach expresses himself in different ways. At one time he sees no utility in employing the ordinary abstractions: "We know *only* of sensations, and the assumption of those nuclei (particles of matter) and their mutual actions as the assigned origins of sensations, shows itself entirely futile and superfluous."[56] Another time he does not wish to discredit the common view of unsophisticated "naive realism," because it renders great services to mankind in their common life. It has grown as a product of nature, whereas every philosophical system is an ephemeral product of art, for temporary aims. So we have to see "why and to what purposes we usually take one point of view, and why and to what purpose we *temporarily* give it up. No point of view holds absolutely; each imports for special aims only."[57]

In the practical application of his views upon physics Mach met with little success. His campaign was chiefly directed against matter and atoms dominating physical science. Not simply because they are and should be acknowledged as abstractions: "Atoms we can observe nowhere, they are as every substance products of thought," but because they are impractical abstractions. They mean an attempt to reduce all physics to mechanics, to the motion of small particles, "and it is easy to see that by mechanical hypotheses a real economy of scientific thought cannot be achieved."[58] But his criticism of heat as a form of motion of small particles, already in 1873, and of electricity as a streaming fluid, found no echo among physicists. On the contrary these explanations developed in ever wider applications, and their consequences were confirmed ever again; atomic theory could boast of ever more results and was extended even to electricity in the theory of electrons. Hence the generation of physicists that followed him, while sympathizing with his general views and accepting them, did not follow him in his special applications. Only in the new century, when atomic and electronic theory had progressed in a brilliant display, and when the theory of relativity arose, there appeared a host of glaring contradictions in which Mach's principles showed themselves the best guides in clearing up the difficulties.

Avenarius

The title of Lenin's work *Materialism and Empirio–criticism* imposes the necessity to treat here the Zürich philosopher Richard Avenarius, because empirio–criticism was the name he gave to his doctrine, in many parts touching upon Mach's views. In his chief work *Kritik der reinen Erfahrung* (Criticism of Pure Experience) he starts from simple experience, considers carefully what is certain about it, and then tests critically what man derived and assumed about the world and himself, what is tenable and justifiable in it and what is not.[59]

In the natural worldview, he explains, I find the following things. I find myself with thoughts and feelings within a surrounding world; to these surroundings belong fellow–men acting and speaking as I do, whom therefore I assume to be similar to myself. Strictly speaking, the interpretation of the movements and sounds connected with fellow–man as having a meaning just as mine is an assumption, not a real experience. But it is a necessary assumption without which a reasonable worldview would be impossible: "the empirio–critical basic assumption of human equality."[60] Then this is my world: first my own statements, e.g., 'I see (or touch) a tree' (I call this an observation) ; I find it, repeatedly, back at the same spot, I describe it as an object in space; I call it 'world', distinct from myself, or 'outer world.' Moreover I have remembrances (I call them ideas), somehow analogous to observations. Secondly there are fellow–men as part of the world. Thirdly there are statements of the fellow–men dealing with the same world; he speaks to me of the tree he, too, is seeing; what he says clearly depends on the 'world.' So far all is simple and natural, there is nothing more to have thoughts about, nothing of inner and outer, of soul and body.

Now, however, I say: my world is object of the observation of my fellow–man; he is the bearer of the observation, it is part of him; I put it into him, and so I do with his other experiences, thoughts, feelings, of which I know through his sayings. I say that he has an 'impression' of the tree, that he makes himself a 'conception' of the tree. An impression, a conception, a sensation of another person, however, is imperceptible to me; it finds no place in my world of experience. By so doing I introduce something that has a new character, that can never be experience to me, that is entirely foreign to all that so far was present. Thus my fellow–man has now got an inner world of observations, feelings, knowledge, and an outer world that he observes and knows. Since I stand to him as he stands to me I too have an inner world of sensations and feelings opposite to that which I call the 'outer' world. The tree I saw and know is split into knowledge and an object. This process is called 'introjection' by Avenarius; something is introduced, introjected into man that was not present in the original simple empirical world conception.

Introjection has made a cleavage in the world. It is the philosophical fall of man. Before the fall he was in a state of philosophical innocence; he took the world as simple, single, as the senses show it; he did not know of body and soul, of mind and matter, of good and evil. The introjection brought dualism with all its problems and contradictions. Let us look at its consequences already at the lowest state of civilization. On the basis of experience introjection takes place not only into fellow–man but also into fellow–animals, into fellow–things, into trees, rocks, etc.: this is animism. We see a man sleeping; awakened he says he was elsewhere; so part of him rested here, part left the body temporarily. If it does not return, the first part is rotting away, but the other part appears in dreams, ghostly. So man consists of a perishable body and a non–perishing spirit. Such spirits also live in trees, in the air, in heaven. At a higher stage of civilization the direct experience of spirits disappears; what is experienced is the outer world of senses; the inner spiritual world is super–sensual. "Experience as things and experience as knowledge now stand against one another, incomparable as a material and a spiritual world."[61]

In this short summary of Avenarius' exposure of his views we omitted one thing that to him is an essential link in the chain. To the sayings of the fellow–man belongs not only himself and his body, but belongs in particular his brain. In my experience, Avenarius says, I have three dependencies: between the sayings of man and his outer world, between his brain and the outer world, and between his brain and his sayings. The second is a physical relation, part of the law of energy; the other two belong to logic.

Avenarius now proceeds first to criticize and then to eliminate introjection. That actions and sayings of fellow–men are related to the outer world is my experience. When I introduce it as ideas into him, it is into his brain that I introduce them. But no anatomical section can disclose them. "We cannot find any characteristic in the thought or in the brain to show that thought is a part or character of the brain."[62] Man can say truly: I have brain; i.e., to the complex called "myself" brain belongs as a part; he can say truly: I have thoughts, i.e., to the complex "myself" thoughts belong as a part. But that does not imply that my brain has these thoughts. "Thought is thought of myself, but not therefore thought of my brain . . . . Brain is no lodging or site, no producer, no instrument or organ, no bearer or substratum, etc., of thinking . . . . Thinking is no resident or commander, no other side, no product either, not even a physiological function of the brain."[63]

This imposing enumeration of usual psychological statements discloses why the brain was introduced. To refute our introjection of a mental world into fellow–man, Avenarius emphasizes that its place would then be the brain, and the brain when anatomically dissected does not show it. Elsewhere he says: introjection means that my thinking puts itself at the place of fellow–man, hence my thinking combines with his brain, which can be done only in fantasy, not really. As arguments to serve as the basis of a philosophical system they are rather artificial and unconvincing. What is true and important is the disclosure of the fact of introjection, the demonstration that in our assumption that the world of fellow–man is the same kind of thing as my own, I introduce a second world of fantasy of another character, entirely outside my experience. It corresponds point for point with my own; its introduction is necessary; but it means a doubling of the world, or rather a multiplication of worlds not directly accessible to me, no possible part of my world of experience.

Now Avenarius sees as his task the building up of a world–structure free from introjection, by means of the simple data of experience. In his exposition he finds it necessary to introduce a special system of new names, characters and figures with algebraic expressions to designate our ordinary concepts. The laudable intention is this; not to be led astray by instinctive associations and meanings connected with ordinary language. But the result is an appearance of profoundness with an abstruse terminology that needs to be back–translated into our usual terms if we want to understand its meanings, and is a source of easy misunderstandings. His argument expressed thus by himself in a far more intricate way, may be summarized as follows:

We find ourselves, a relative constant, amidst a changing multitude of units denoted as 'trees', 'fellow–men', etc., which show many mutual relations. 'Myself' and 'surroundings' are found both at the same time in the same experience; we call them 'central–part' and 'counter–part' (*Zentralglied und Gegenglied*). That my fellow–man has thoughts, experiences, and a world just as I have, is expressed in the statement that part of my surroundings is central–part itself. When in his brain variations take place (they belong to my world of experience), then phenomena occur in his world; his sayings about them are determined by processes in his brains. In my world of experience the outer world determines the change in his brain (a neurological fact); not my observed tree determines his observation (situated in another world), but the changes caused by the tree in his brain (both belonging to my world) determine his observation. Now my scientific experience declares my brain and his brain to change in the same way through impressions of the outer world; hence the resulting 'his world' and my world must be of the same stuff. So the natural world–conception is restored without the need of introjection. The argument comes down to this that our practice of assuming similar thoughts and conceptions as our own in fellow–men, which should be illicit notwithstanding our spiritual intercourse, should become valid as soon as we make a detour along the material brains. To which must be remarked that neurology may assume as a valid theory that the outer world produces the same changes in my brain and in another man's; but that, strictly keeping to my experience, I have never observed it and never can observe it.

Avenarius' ideas have nothing in common with Dietzgen; they do not deal with the connection between knowledge and experience. They are cognate to Mach's in that both proceed from experience, dissolve the entire world into experience, and believe thus to have done away with dualism.

> If we keep 'complete experience' free from all adulteration, . . . our world–conception will be free from all metaphysical dualism. To these eliminated dualisms belong the absolute antithesis of 'body' and 'mind', of 'matter' and 'spirit', in short of physical and psychical . . . . Things physical, matter in its metaphysical absolute sense finds no place in purified 'complete experience', because 'matter' in this conception is only an abstractum, indicating the entirety of counter–parts when abstraction is made of all 'central–parts.'[64]

This is analogous to Mach; but it is different from Mach in being built out into a finished and closed system. The equality of the experience of fellow–man, settled by Mach in a few words, is a most difficult piece of work to Avenarius. The neutral character of the elements of experience is pointed out with more precision by Avenarius; they are no sensations, nothing psychical, but simply something 'found present' (*Vorgefundenes*).

So he opposes prevailing psychology, that formerly dealt with the 'soul', afterwards with 'psychic functions', because it proceeds from the assumption that the observed world is an image within us. This, he says, is not a "thing found present," and neither can it be disclosed from what is "found present."

> Whereas I leave the tree before me as something seen in the same relation to me, as a thing 'found present' to me, prevailing psychology puts the tree as 'something seen' into man, especially into his brain . . . . Introjection created this false object of psychology; it changed 'before me' into 'in me', what is 'found present' into what is 'imagined'; it made 'part of (real) surroundings' into 'part of (ideal) thinking.'[65]

For Avenarius, instead, the material changes in the brain are the basis of psychology. He proceeds from the thesis taken over from the special science of physiology that all action of the surroundings produces changes in the brain and that these produce thoughts and sayings—and this certainly lies outside direct experience. It is a curious fact that Mach and Carnap too speak of observing (ideally, not really) the brain (by physical or chemical methods, or by a 'brain–mirror') to see what happens there in connection with sensations and thoughts. It seems that middle–class theory of knowledge cannot do without having recourse to this materialist conception. Avenarius is the most radical in this respect; for him psychology is the science of the dependence of behavior upon the brain; what belongs to the actions of man is not psychical but physiological, mere brain processes. When we speak of ideas and ideologies, empirio–criticism speaks of changes in the central nervous system. The study of the great world–moving ideas in the history of mankind turns into the study of their nervous systems. Thus empirio–criticism stands close to middle–class materialism that also, in the problem of the determination of ideas by the surrounding world, appeals to brain–matter. In comparing Avenarius with Haeckel we should rather call him Haeckel reversed. Both can understand mind only as an attribute of the brain; since mind and matter, however, are fundamentally disparate, Haeckel attributes a particle of mind to every atom, whereas Avenarius entirely dispenses with the mind, as a special something. But therefore the world for him takes instead the somewhat shadowy character—frightening to materialists and opening the gate to ideological interpretations—of consisting of 'my experience' only.

Right as Avenarius may be that it is not strictly experience, the equalization of fellow–men with ourselves and the identity of their world with ours is an inevitable natural affair, whatever kind of spiritual or material terms are used to express it. The point is again that middle–class philosophy wants to criticize and correct human thinking instead of trying to understand it as a natural process.

In this context a general remark must be made. The essential character in Mach and Avenarius, as in most modern philosophers of science, is that they start from personal experience. It is their only basis of certainty; to it they go back when asked what is true. When fellow–men enter into the play, a kind of theoretical uncertainty appears, and with difficult reasonings their experience must be reduced to ours. We have here an effect of the strong individualism of the middle–class world. The middle–class individual in his strong feeling of personality has lost social consciousness; he does not know how entirely he is a social being. In everything of himself, in his body, his mind, his life, his thoughts, his feeling, in his most simple experiences he is a product of society; human society made them all what they are. What is considered a purely personal sensation: 'I see a tree'—can enter into consciousness only through the distinctness given to it by names. Without the inherited words to indicate things and species, actions and concepts, the sensation could not be expressed and conceived. Out of the indistinctive mass of the world of impressions the important parts come forward only when they are denoted by sounds and thus become separated from the unimportant mass. When Carnap constructs the world without using the old names, he still makes use of his capacity of abstract thinking. Abstract thinking, however, by means of concepts, is not possible without speech; speech and abstract thinking developed together as a product of society.

Speech could never have originated without human society for which it is an organ of mutual communication. It could develop in a society only, as an instrument in the practical activity of man. This activity is a social process that as the deepest foundation underlies all my experiences. The activity of fellow–man, inclusive of his speaking, I experience as co–natural with my activity because they are parts of one common activity; thus we know our similarity. Man is first an active being, a worker. To live he must eat, i.e., he must seize and assimilate other things; he must search, fight, conquer. This action upon the world, a life–necessity, determines his thinking and feeling, because it is his chief life content and forms the most essential parts of his experiences. It was from the first a collective activity, a social labor process. Speech originated as part of this collective process, as an indispensable mediator in the common work, and at the same time as an instrument of reflexive thinking needed in the handling of tools, themselves products of collective working. In such a way the entire world of experience of man bears a social character. The simple 'natural world view' taken by Avenarius and other philosophers as their starting point, is not the spontaneous view of a primitive single man but, in philosophical garb, the outcome of a highly developed society.

Social development has, through the increasing division of labor, dissected and separated what before was a unit. Scientists and philosophers have the special task of investigating and reasoning so that their science and their conceptions may play their role in the total process of production—now the role chiefly of supporting and strengthening the existing social system. Cut off from the root of life, the social process of labor, they hang in the air and have to resort to artificial reasonings to find a basis. Thus the philosopher starts with imagining himself the only being on earth and suspiciously asks whether he can demonstrate his own existence, until he is happily reassured by Descartes' "I think, so I exist." Then along a chain of logical deductions he proceeds to ascertain the existence of the world and of fellow–men; and so the self–evident comes out along a wide detour—if it comes out. For the middle–class philosopher does not feel the necessity to follow up to the last consequences, to material-ism, and he prefers to stay somewhere in–between, expressing the world in ideological terms.

So this is the difference: middle–class philosophy looks for the source of knowledge in personal meditation, Marxism finds it in social la-bor. All consciousness, all spiritual life of man, even of the most lonely hermit, is a collective product, has been made and shaped by the working community of mankind. Though in the form of personal consciousness—because man is a biological individual—it can exist only as part of the whole. People can have experiences only as social beings; though the contents are personally different, in their essence experiences are super–personal, society being their self–evident ba-sis. Thus the objective world of phenomena which logical thought constructs out of the data of experience, is first and foremost, by its origin already, collective experience of mankind.

Lenin

How Mach's ideas could acquire importance in the Russian socialist movement may be understood from social conditions. The young Russian intelligentsia, owing to the barbarous pre–capitalist conditions, had not yet, as in Western Europe, found its social function in the service of a bourgeoisie. So it had to aspire for the downfall of Czarism, and to join the socialist party. At the same time it stood in spiritual intercourse with the Western intellectuals and so took part in the spiritual trends of the Western world. Thus it was inevitable that efforts should be made to combine them with Marxism.

Of course Lenin had to oppose these tendencies. Marxian theory, indeed, can gain nothing essential from Mach. Insofar as a better understanding of human thinking is needed for socialists, this can be found in Dietzgen's work. Mach was significant because he deduced analogous ideas out of the practices of natural science, for the use of scientists. In what he has in common with Dietzgen, the reduction of the world to experience, he stopped midway and gave, imbued with the anti–materialist trends of his time, a vague idealistic form to his views. This could not be grafted upon Marxism. Here Marxist criticism was needed.

The Criticism

Lenin, however in attacking Mach, from the start presents the antagonism in a wrong way. Proceeding from a quotation of Engels, he says:

> But the question here is not of this or that formulation of
> materialism, but of the opposition of materialism to idealism, of
> the difference between the two fundamental lines in philosophy.
> Are we to proceed from things to sensation and thought? Or are we
> to proceed from thought and sensation to things? The first line, i.e.,
> the materialist line, is adopted by Engels. The second line, i.e., the
> idealist line, is adopted by Mach.[66]

It is at once clear that this is not the true expression of the antithesis. According to materialism the material world produces thought, consciousness, mind, all things spiritual. That, on the contrary, the spiritual produces the material world, is taught by religion, is found with Hegel, but is not Mach's opinion. The expression "to proceed from . . . to . . ." is used to intermix two quite different meanings. Proceeding from things to sensations and thought means: things create thoughts. Proceeding—not from thoughts to things, as Lenin wrongly imputes to Mach but—from sensations to things, means that only through sensations we arrive at the knowledge of things. Their entire existence is built up out of sensations; to emphasize this truth Mach says: they consist of sensations.

Here the method followed by Lenin in his controversy makes its appearance; he tries to assign to Mach opinions different from the real ones. Especially the doctrine of solipsism. Thus he continues:

> No evasions, no sophisms (a multitude of which we shall yet
> encounter) can remove the clear and indisputable fact that Ernst
> Mach's doctrine of things as complexes of sensations is subjective
> idealism and a simple rehash of Berkeleyanism. If bodies are
> 'complexes of sensations,' as Mach says or 'combinations of sensations,' as Berkeley said, it inevitably follows that the whole world
> is but my idea. Starting from such a premise it is impossible to arrive
> at the existence of other people besides oneself: it is the purest
> solipsism. Much as Mach, Avenarius, Petzoldt, and the others may
> abjure solipsism, they cannot in fact escape solipsism without
> falling into howling logical absurdities.[67]

Now, if anything can be asserted beyond any doubt about Mach and Avenarius, it is that their opinions are not solipsism; fellow–men similar to myself, deduced with more or less stringent logic, are the basis of their world–conception. Lenin, however, manifestly does not care about what Mach really thinks, but about what he should think if his logic were identical with Lenin's.

> From which there is only one possible inference, namely, that the 'world consists only of my sensations.' The word 'our' employed by Mach instead of 'my' is employed illegitimately.[68]

That indeed is an easy way of arguing: what I write down as the opinion of my adversary he replaces unjustifiably by what he wrote down himself. Lenin, moreover, knows quite well that Mach speaks of the objective reality of the world, and himself gives numerous quotations to that effect. But he does not let himself be deceived as so many others were deceived by Mach.

> Similarly, even Mach . . . frequently strays into a materialist interpretation of the word 'experience' . . . . Here nature is taken as primary and sensation and experience as products. Had Mach consistently adhered to his point of view in the fundamental questions of epistemology . . . Mach's special 'philosophy' is here thrown overboard, and the author instinctively accepts the customary standpoint of the scientists.[69]

Would it not have been better if he had tried to understand in what sense it was that Mach assumes that things consist of sensations?

The 'elements' also are an object of difficulty to Lenin. He summarizes Mach's opinion on the elements in six theses, among which we find, in numbers 3 and 4:

> Elements are divided into the physical and the psychical; the latter is that which depends on the human nerves and the human organism generally; the former does not depend on them; the connection of physical elements and the connection of psychical elements, it is declared, do not exist separately from each other; they exist only in conjunction.[70]

Anybody, even if acquainted only superficially with Mach, can see how he is rendered here in an entirely wrong and meaningless way. What Mach really says is this: every element, though described in many words, is an inseparable unity, which can be part of a complex that we call physical, but which combined with different other elements can form a complex that we call psychical. When I feel the heat of a flame, this sensation together with others on heat and thermometers and with visible phenomena combines into the complex 'flame' or 'heat', treated in physics. Combined with other sensations of pain and pleasure, with remembrances and with observations on nerves, the context belongs to physiology or psychology. "None (of these connections) is the only existing one, both are present at the same time," says Mach.[71] For they are the same elements in different combinations. Lenin makes of this that the connections are not independent and only exist together. Mach does not separate the elements themselves in[to] physical and psychical ones, nor does he distinguish a physical and psychical part in them; the same element is physical in one context, psychical in another. If Lenin renders these ideas in such a sloppy and unintelligible way it is no wonder that he cannot make any sense out of it, and speaks of "an incoherent jumble of antithetical philosophical points of view."[72] If one does not take the pains or is unable to unravel the real opinions of his adversary and only snatches up some sentences to interpret them from one's own point of view, he should not wonder that nonsense comes out. This cannot be called a Marxian criticism of Mach.

In the same faulty way he renders Avenarius. He reproduces a small summary by Avenarius of a first division of the elements: what I find present I partly call outer world (e.g., 'I see a tree'), partly not ('I remember a tree, think of a tree'). Avenarius denotes them as thing–like (*sachhaft*) and thought–like (*gedankenhaft*) elements.[73] Thereupon Lenin indignantly exclaims:

> At first we are assured that the 'elements' are something new, both physical and psychical at the same time; then a little correction is surreptitiously inserted: instead of the crude, materialist differentiation of matter (bodies, things) and the psychical (sensations, recollections, fantasies) we are presented with the doctrine of

'recent positivism' regarding elements substantial and elements mental.[74]

Clearly he does not suspect how completely he misses the point.

In a chapter superscribed with the ironical title "Does man think with his brain?" Lenin quotes Avenarius' statement that the brain is not the lodging, the site, etc., of thinking; thinking is no resident, no product, etc., of the brain.[75] Hence: man does not think with his brain. Lenin has not perceived that Avenarius further on expresses clearly enough, though garbed in his artificial terminology, that the action of the outer world upon the brain produces what we call thoughts; manifestly Lenin had not the patience to unravel Avenarius' intricate language. But to combat an opponent you have to know his point; ignorance is no argument. What Avenarius contradicts is not the role of the brain but that we call the product thought when we assign to it, as a spiritual being, a site in the brain and say it is living in the brain, is commanding the brain, or is a function of the brain. The material brain, as we saw, occupies precisely the central place of his philosophy. Lenin, however, considers this only as a "mystification":

> Avenarius here acts on the advice of the charlatan in Turgenev: denounce most of all those vices which you yourself possess. Avenarius tries to pretend that he is combating idealism . . . . While distracting the attention of the reader by attacking idealism, Avenarius is in fact defending idealism, albeit in slightly different words: thought is not a function of the brain; the brain is not the organ of thought; sensations are—not functions of the nervous system, oh, no! sensations are—'elements.'[76]

The critic rages here against a self–mystification without any basis. He finds "idealism" in that Avenarius proceeds from elements, and elements are sensations. Avenarius, however, does not proceed from sensations but from what simple unsophisticated man finds present: things, surroundings, a world, fellow–men, and remembrances. Man does not find present sensations, he finds present a world. Avenarius tries to construct a description of the world without the common language of matter and mind and its contradictions. He finds trees present, and human brains, and—so he believes—changes in the brains produced by the trees, and actions and talk of fellow–men determined by these changes. Of all this Lenin manifestly has no inkling. He tries to make "idealism" of Avenarius' system by considering Avenarius' starting point, experience, to be sensations, something psychical, according to his own materialist view. His error is that he takes the contradistinction materialism/idealism in the sense of middle–class materialism, with physical matter as its basis. Thus he shuts himself off completely from any understanding of modern views that proceed from experience and phenomena as the given reality.

Lenin now brings forward an array of witnesses to declare that the doctrines of Mach and Avenarius are idealism or solipsism. It is natural that the host of professional philosophers, in compliance with the tendency of bourgeois thinking to proclaim the rule of mind over matter, try to interpret and emphasize the anti–materialist side of their ideas; they too know materialism only as the doctrine of physical matter. What, we may ask, is the use of such witnesses? When disputed facts have to be ascertained, witnesses are necessary. When, however, we deal with the understanding of somebody's opinions and theories, we have to read and render carefully what he himself has written to expound them; this is the only way to find out similarities and differences, truth and error. For Lenin, however, matters were different. His book was part of a lawsuit, an act of impeachment; as such it required an array of witnesses. An important political issue was at stake; Machism threatened to corrupt the fundamental doctrines, the theoretical unity of the Party; so its spokesmen had to do away with them. Mach and Avenarius formed a danger for the Party; hence what mattered was not to find out what was true and valuable in their teachings in order to widen our own views. What mattered was to discredit them, to destroy their reputation, to reveal them as muddle–heads contradicting themselves, speaking confused fudge, trying to hide their real opinions and not believing their own assertions.

All the middle–class philosophical writers, standing before the newness of these ideas, look for analogies and relationships of Mach and Avenarius with former philosophic systems; one welcomes Mach as fitting in with Kant, another sees a likeness to Hume, or Berkeley, or Fichte. In this multitude and variety of systems it is easy to find out connections and similarities everywhere. Lenin registers all such contradictory judgments and in this way demonstrates Mach's confusion. The like with Avenarius. For instance:

> And it is difficult to say who more rudely unmasks Avenarius the mystifier—Smith by his straightforward and clear refutation, or Schuppe by his enthusiastic opinion of Avenarius' crowning work. The kiss of Wilhelm Schuppe in philosophy is no better than the kiss of Peter Struve or Menshikov in politics.[77]

If we now read Schuppe's "Open Letter to Avenarius," in which in flattering words he expresses his agreement, we find that he did not at all grasp the essence of Avenarius' opinion; he takes the 'myself' as the starting point instead of the elements found present, out of which Avenarius constructs the 'myself.'[78] He misrepresents Avenarius in the same way as Lenin does, with this difference, that what displeased Lenin pleased him. In his answer Avenarius, in the courteous words usual among scholars, testifies to his satisfaction at the assent of such a famous thinker, but then again expounds the real contents of his doctrine. Lenin neglects the contents of these explanations which refute his conclusions, and quotes only the compromising courtesies.

Natural Science

Over against Mach's ideas Lenin puts the materialistic views, the objective reality of the material world, of matter, light–ether, laws of nature, such as natural science and human common sense accept. These last are two respectable authorities; but in this case their weight is not very great. Lenin sneeringly quotes Mach's own confession that he found little consent among his colleagues. A critic, however, who brings new ideas cannot be refuted by the statement that it is the old criticized ideas that are generally accepted. And as to common sense, i.e., the totality of opinions of uninstructed people: they usually represent the dicta of science of a former period, that gradually, by teaching and popular books, seeped down the masses. That the earth revolves around the sun, that the world consists of indestructible matter, that matter consists of atoms, that the world is eternal and infinite—all this has gradually penetrated into the minds, first of the educated classes, then of the masses. When science proceeds to newer and better views, all this old knowledge can, as 'common sense', be brought forward against them.

How unsuspectingly Lenin leans upon these two authorities—and even in a wrong way—is seen when he says:

> For every scientist who has not been led astray by professorial philosophy, as well as for every materialist, sensation is indeed the direct connection between consciousness and the external world; it is the transformation of the energy of external excitation into a state of consciousness. This transformation has been, and is, observed by each of us a million times an every hand.[79]

This 'observing' is of the same kind as when one should say: 'We see a thousand times that our eye sees and that light falls upon the retina.' In reality we do not see our seeing and our retina; we see objects and infer the retina and the seeing. We do not observe energy and its transitions; we observe phenomena, and out of these phenomena physicists have abstracted the concept of energy. The transformation of energy is a summarized physical expression for the many phenomena in which one measured quantity decreased, another increased. They are all good expedient concepts and inferences, reliable in the prediction of future phenomena, and so we call them true. Lenin takes this truth in such an absolute way that he thinks he expresses an observed fact 'adopted by every materialist', when he pronounces what is actually a physical theory. Moreover his exposition is wrong. That energy of the light–impression is converted into consciousness may have been the belief of middle–class materialists, but science does not know of it. Physical science says that energy transforms exclusively, and completely, into other energy; the energy of the light–impression is transformed into other forms: chemical, electrical, heat–energy; but consciousness is not known in physics as a form of energy.

This confounding of the real, observed world and the physical concepts permeates Lenin's work on every page. Engels denoted materialists as those who considered nature the original thing. Lenin speaks of a "materialism which regards nature, matter, as primary."[80] And in another place: "matter is the objective reality given to us in sensations."[81] To Lenin nature and physical matter are identical; the name matter has the same meaning as objective world. In this he agrees with middle–class materialism that in the same way considers matter as the real substance of the world. Thus his angry polemics against Mach can be easily understood. To Mach matter is an abstract concept formed out of the phenomena—or more strictly: sensations. So Lenin, now finding the denial of the reality of matter, then reading the simple statement of the reality of the world, sees only confusion; and he pretends, now, that Mach is a solipsist and denies the existence of the world, and then scornfully remarks that Mach throws his own philosophy to the winds and returns to scientific views.

With the laws of nature the case is analogous. Mach's opinion that cause and effect as well as natural laws do not factually exist in nature, but are man–made expressions of observed regularities, is asserted by Lenin to be identical with Kant's doctrine.

> It is man who dictates laws to nature and not nature that dictates laws to man! The important thing is not the repetition of Kant's doctrine of apriorism . . . but the fact that reason, mind, consciousness are here primary, and nature secondary. It is not reason that is a part of nature, one of its highest products, the reflection of its processes, but nature that is a part of reason, which thereby is stretched from the ordinary, simple human reason known to us all to a 'stupendous,' as Dietzgen puts it, mysterious, divine reason. The Kantian–Machian formula, that 'man gives laws to nature,' is a fideist formula.[82]

This confused tirade, entirely missing the point, can only be understood if we consider that for Lenin 'nature' consists not only in matter but also in natural laws directing its behavior, floating somehow in the world as commanders who must be obeyed by the things.

Hence to deny the objective existence of these laws means to him the denial of nature itself; to make man the creator of natural laws means to him to make human mind the creator of the world. How then the logical salto is made to the deity as the creator must remain an enigma to the unsophisticated reader.

Two pages earlier he writes:

> The really important epistemological question that divides the philosophical trends is . . . whether the source of our knowledge of these connections is objective natural law or properties of our mind, its innate faculty of apprehending certain a priori truths, and so forth. This is what so irrevocably divides the materialists Feuerbach, Marx, and Engels from the agnostic (Humeans) Avenarius and Mach.[83]

That Mach should ascribe to the human mind the power to disclose certain aprioristic truths is a new discovery or rather fantasy of Lenin. Where Mach deals with the practice of the mind to abstract general rules from experience and to assign to them unlimited validity, Lenin, captivated by traditional philosophical ideas, thinks of disclosing aprioristic truths. Then he continues:

> In certain parts of his works, Mach . . . frequently 'forgets' his agreement with Hume and his own subjectivist theory of causality and argues 'simply' as a scientist, i.e., from the instinctive materialist standpoint. For instance, in his *Mechanik* we read of the 'uniformity . . . which nature teaches us to find in its phenomena.' But if we do find uniformity in the phenomena of nature, does this mean that uniformity exists objectively outside our mind? No. On the question of the uniformity of nature Mach also delivers himself thus: . . . 'That we consider ourselves capable of making predictions with the help of such a law only proves that there is sufficient uniformity in our environment, but it does not prove the necessity of the success of our predictions.' It follows that we may and ought to look for a necessity apart from the uniformity of our environment, i.e., of nature.[84]

The embroilment in this tangle of sentences, further embellished by courtesies here omitted, is understandable only when conformity of nature is identical for Lenin with the necessity of success of our prophecies; when, hence, he cannot distinguish between regularities as they occur in various degrees of clearness in nature, and the apodictic expression of exact natural law. And he proceeds:

> Where to look for it is the secret of idealist philosophy which is afraid to recognize man's perceptive faculty as a simple reflection of nature.[85]

In reality there is no necessity, except in our formulation of natural law; and then in practice ever again we find deviations, which, again, we express in the form of additional laws. Natural law does not determine what nature necessarily will do, but what we expect her to do. The silly remark that our mind should simply reflect nature we may leave undiscussed now. His concluding remark:

> In his last work, *Erkenntnis und Irrtum*, Mach even defines a law of nature as a 'limitation of expectation'! Solipsism claims its own.[86]

This lacks all sense since the determination of our expectation by natural law is a common affair of all scientists. The embodiment of a number of phenomena in a short formula, a natural law, is denoted by Mach as 'economy of thinking'; he exalts it into a principle of research. We might expect that such a reducing of abstract theory to the practice of (scientific) labor should find sympathy among Marxists. In Lenin, however, it meets with no response, and he exposes his lack of understanding in some drolleries:

> That it is more 'economical' to 'think' that only I and my sensations exist is unquestionable, provided we want to introduce such an absurd conception into epistemology. Is it 'more economical' to 'think' of the atom as indivisible, or as composed of positive and negative electrons? Is it 'more economical' to think of the Russian bourgeois revolution as being conducted by the liberals or as being conducted against the liberals? One has only to put the question in order to see the absurdity, the subjectivism of applying the category of 'the economy of thought' here.[87]

And he opposes to it his own view:

> Human thought is 'economical' only when it correctly reflects
> objective truth, and the criterion of this correctness is practice,
> experiment and industry. Only by denying objective reality, that is,
> by denying the foundations of Marxism, can one seriously speak of
> economy of thought in the theory of knowledge.[88]

How simple and evident that looks. Let us take an example. The
old Ptolemaic world–system placed the earth as resting in the center
of the world, with the sun and the planets revolving around it, the
latter in epicycles, a combination of two circles. Copernicus placed
the sun in the center and had the earth and the planets revolving
around it in simple circles. The visible phenomena are exactly the
same after both theories, because we can observe the relative motions
only, and they are absolutely identical. Which, then, pictures the
objective world in the right way? Practical experience cannot distinguish between them; the predictions are identical. Copernicus pointed
to the fixed stars which by the parallax could give a decision; but in
the old theory we could have the stars making a yearly circle just as
the planets did; and again both theories give identical results. But
then everybody will say: it is absurd to have all those thousands of
bodies describe similar circles, simply to keep the earth at rest. Why
absurd? Because it makes our world–picture needlessly complicated.
Here we have it: the Copernican system is chosen and stated to be
true because it gives the most simple world system. This example
may suffice to show the naiveté of the idea that we choose a theory
because after the criterion of experience it pictures reality rightly.

Kirchhoff has formulated the real character of scientific theory in
the same way by his well–known statement that mechanics, instead
of "explaining" motions by means of the "forces" producing them,
has the task "to describe the motions in nature in the most complete
and simple way."[89] Thus the fetishism of forces as causes, as a kind of
working imps, was removed; they are a short form of description
only. Mach of course pointed to the analogy of Kirchhoff's views and
his own. Lenin, to show that he does not understand anything of it,
because he is entirely captivated in this fetishism, calls out in an in-

dignant tone: "'Economy of thought,' from which Mach in 1872 inferred that sensations alone exist, . . . is declared to be . . . equivalent to the simplest description (of an objective reality, the existence of which it never occurred to Kirchhoff to doubt!)."[90]

It must be remarked, besides, that thinking never can picture reality completely; theory is an approximate picture that renders only the main features, the general traits of a group of phenomena.

After having considered Lenin's ideas on matter and natural laws, we take as a third instance space and time.

> Behold now the 'teachings' of 'recent positivism' on this subject. We read in Mach: 'Space and time are well ordered (*wohlgeordnete*) systems of series of sensations.' This is palpable idealist nonsense, such as inevitably follows from the doctrine that bodies are complexes of sensations. According to Mach, it is not man with his sensations that exists in space and time, but space and time that exist in man, that depend upon man and are generated by man. He feels that he is falling into idealism, and 'resists' by making a host of reservations and . . . burying the question under lengthy disquisitions . . . on the mutability of our conceptions of space and time. But this does not save him, and cannot save him, for one can really overcome the idealist position on this question only by recognizing the objective reality of space and time. And this Mach will not do at any price. He constructs his epistemological theory of time and space on the principle of relativism, and that is all . . . . Resisting the idealist conclusions which inevitably follow from his premises, Mach argues against Kant and insists that our conception of space is derived from experience. But if objective reality is not given us in experience (as Mach teaches) . . .[91]

What is the use of going on quoting? It is all a sham battle, because we know that Mach assumes the reality of the world; and all phenomena, constituting the world, take place in space and time. And Lenin could have been warned that he was on a false track, by a number of sentences he knows and partly quotes, where Mach discusses the mathematical investigations on multi–dimensional spaces. There Mach says: "That which we call space is a special real case among more general imagined cases . . . . The space of vision and

touch is a threefold manifold, it has three dimensions . . . . The properties of given space appear directly as objects of experience . . . .
About the given space only experience can teach us whether it is
finite, whether parallel lines intersect, etc. . . . . To many divines who
do not know where to place hell, and to spiritualists, a fourth dimension might be very convenient." But "such a fourth dimension would
still remain a thing of imagination."[92] These quotations may suffice.
What has Lenin to say to all this, besides a number of groundless
squibs and invectives?

> But how does he (Mach) dissociate himself from them in his theory
> of knowledge? By stating that three–dimensional space alone is
> real! But what sort of defense is it against the theologians and their
> like when you deny objective reality to space and time?[93]

What difference might there be between real space and objective
reality of space? At any rate he sticks to his error.

What, then, is that sentence of Mach that was the basis of this
fantasy? In the last chapter of his *Mechanik*, Mach discusses the relation between different branches of science. There he says: "First we
perceive that in all experiences of spatial and temporal relations we
have more confidence, and a more objective and real character is
ascribed to them, than to experiences on color, heat or sound . . . .
Yet, looking more exactly, we cannot fail to see that sensations on
space and time are sensations just as those of color, sound or smell;
only, in the former we are more trained and clear than in the latter.
Space and time are well–ordered systems of series of sensations . . . ."[94]
Mach proceeds here from experience; our sensations are the only
source of knowledge; our entire world, including all we know about
space and time, is built up out of them.

The question of what is the meaning of absolute space and time is
to Mach a meaningless question; the only sensible question is how
space and time appear in our experience. Just as with bodies and
matter we can form a scientific conception of time and space only
through abstraction out of the totality of our experiences. With the
space–and–time pattern in which we insert these experiences we are
versed, as most simple and natural, from early youth. How it then

appears in experimental science cannot be expressed in a better way than by the words of Mach: well–ordered systems of series of experiences.

What, contrariwise, Lenin thinks of space and time, transpires from the following quotation:

> In modern physics, he says, Newton's idea of absolute time and space prevails, of time and space as such. This idea seems 'to us' senseless, Mach continues—apparently not suspecting the existence of materialists and of a materialist theory of knowledge. But in practice, he claims, this view was harmless (*unschädlich*) and therefore for a long time escaped criticism.[95]

Hence, according to Lenin, "materialism" accepts Newton's doctrine, the basis of which is that there exists an absolute space and an absolute time. This means that the place in space is fixed absolutely, without regard to other things, and can be ascertained without any doubt. When Mach says that this is the point of view of contemporary physicists he surely represents his colleagues as too old–fashioned; in his time already it was rather generally accepted that motion and rest were relative conceptions, that the place of a body is always the place relative to other bodies, and that the idea of absolute position has no sense.

Still there was a certain doubt whether or not space–filling world–ether did not offer a frame for absolute space; motion or rest relative to world–ether could be rightly called then absolute motion or rest. When, however, physicists tried to determine it by means of the propagation of light, they could find nothing but relativity. Such was the case with Michelson's famous experiment in 1889, arranged in such a way that in its result nature should indicate the motion of our earth relative to the ether. But nothing was found; nature remained mute. It was as if she said: your query has no sense. To explain the negative result it was assumed that there always occurred additional phenomena that just canceled the expected effect—until Einstein in 1905 in his theory of relativity combined all facts in such a way that the result was self–evident. Also within the world–occupying ether absolute position was shown to be a word without meaning. So gradually the idea of ether itself was dropped, and all thought of absolute space disappeared from science.

With time it seemed to be different; a moment in time was assumed to be absolute. But it was the very ideas of Mach that brought about a change here. In the place of talk of abstract conceptions, Einstein introduced the practice of experiment. What are we doing when we fix a moment in time? We look at a clock, and we compare the different clocks; there is no other way. In following this line of argument Einstein succeeded in refuting absolute time and demonstrating the relativity of time. Einstein's theory was soon universally adopted by scientists, with the exception of some antisemitic physicists in Germany who consequently were proclaimed luminaries of national–socialist 'German' physics.

The latter development could not yet be known to Lenin when he wrote his book. But it illustrates the character of such expositions as where he writes:

> The materialist view of space and time has remained 'harmless,' i.e., compatible, as heretofore, with science, while the contrary view of Mach and Co. was a 'harmful' capitulation to the position of fideism.[96]

Thus he denotes as materialist the belief that the concepts of absolute space and absolute time, which science once wanted as its theory but had to drop afterwards, are the true reality of the world.[A] Because Mach opposes their reality and asserts for space and time the same as for every concept, viz. that we can deduce them only from experience, Lenin imputes to him 'idealism leading to fideism.'

Materialism

Our direct concern here is not with Mach but with Lenin. Mach occupies considerable space here because Lenin's criticism of Mach discloses his own philosophical views. From the side of Marxism there is enough to criticize in Mach; but Lenin takes up the matter from the wrong end. As we have seen he appeals to the old forms of physical theory, diffused into popular opinion, so as to oppose them against the modern critique of their own foundations. We found, moreover, that he identifies the real objective world with physical matter, as middle–class materialism did formerly. He tries to demonstrate it by the following arguments:

> If you hold that it is given, a philosophical concept is needed for this objective reality, and this concept has been worked out long, long ago. This concept is matter. Matter is a philosophical category designating the objective reality which is given to man by his sensations, and which is copied, photographed and reflected by our sensations, while existing independently of them.[97]

Fine; with the first sentence we all can agree. When then, however, we would restrict the character of reality to physical matter, we contradict the first given definition. Electricity too is objective reality; is it physical matter? Our sensations show us light; it is reality but not matter; and the concepts introduced by the physicists to explain its phenomena, first the world–ether, then the photons, cannot easily be denoted as a kind of matter. Is not energy quite as real as is physical matter? More directly than the material things, it is their energy that shows itself in all experience and produces our sensations. For that reason Ostwald, half a century ago, proclaimed energy the only real substance of the world; and he called this "the end of scientific materialism."[98] And finally, what is given to us in our sensations, when fellow–men speak to us, is not only sound coming from lips and throat, not only energy of air vibrations, but besides, more essentially, their thoughts, their ideas. Man's ideas quite as certainly belong to objective reality as the tangible objects; things spiritual constitute the real world just as things called material in physics. If in our science, needed to direct our activity, we wish to render the entire world of experience, the concept of physical matter does not suffice; we need more and other concepts; energy, mind, consciousness.

If according to the above definition matter is taken as the name for the philosophical concept denoting objective reality, it embraces far more than physical matter. Then we come to the view repeatedly expressed in former chapters, where the material world was spoken of as the name for the entire observed reality. This is the meaning of the word *materia,* matter in Historical Materialism, the designation of all that is really existing in the world, "including mind and fancies," as Dietzgen said.[99] It is not, therefore, that the modern theories of the structure of matter provoke criticism of his ideas, as Lenin indicates above on the same page, but the fact that he identifies physical matter at all with the real world.

The meaning of the word matter in Historical Materialism, as pointed out here, is of course entirely foreign to Lenin; contrary to his first definition he will restrict it to physical matter. Hence his attack on Dietzgen's "confusion":

> Thinking is a function of the brain, says Dietzgen. 'My desk as a picture in my mind is identical with my idea of it. But my desk outside of my brain is a separate object and distinct from my idea.' These perfectly clear materialistic propositions are, however, supplemented by Dietzgen thus: 'Nevertheless, the non–sensible idea is also sensible, material, i.e., real . . . .' This is obviously false. That both thought and matter are 'real,' i.e., exist, is true. But to say that thought is material is to make a false step, a step towards confusing materialism and idealism. As a matter of fact this is only an inexact expression of Dietzgen.[100]

Here Lenin repudiates his own definition of matter as the philosophical expression of objective reality. Or is perhaps objective reality something different from really existing? What he tries to express but cannot without "inexactness of expression"—is this: that thoughts may really exist, but the true genuine reality is only found in physical matter.

Middle–class materialism, identifying objective reality with physical matter, had to make every other reality, such as all things spiritual, an attribute or property of this matter. We cannot wonder, therefore, that we find with Lenin similar ideas. To Pearson's sentence, "It is illogical to assert that all matter has consciousness," he remarks:

It is illogical to assert that all matter is conscious but it is logical to assert that all matter possesses a property which is essentially akin to sensation, the property of reflection.[101]

And still more distinctly he avers against Mach:

As regards materialism, . . . we have already seen in the case of Diderot[B] what the real views of the materialists are. These views do not consist in deriving sensation from the movement of matter or in reducing sensation to the movement of matter, but in recognizing sensation as one of the properties of matter in motion. On this question Engels shared the standpoint of Diderot.[102]

Where Engels may have said so, is not indicated. We may doubt whether Lenin's conviction that Engels on this point agreed with him and Diderot, rests on precise statements. In his *Anti–Dühring* Engels expressed himself in another way: "Life is the form of existence of albuminous substances;" i.e., life is not a property of all matter but appears only in such complicated molecular structures as albumen.[103] So it is not probable that he should have considered sensitiveness, which we know as a property of living matter only, a property of all matter. Such generalizations of properties observed only in special eases, to matter in general, belong to the undialectical middle–class frame of mind.

The remark may be inserted here that Plekhanov exhibits ideas analogous to Lenin's. In his *Grundprobleme des Marxismus* he criticizes the botanist Francè on the subject of the "spirituality of matter," the "doctrine that matter in general and organic matter especially always has a certain sensitivity." Plekhanov then expresses his own view in the words: "Francè considers this contradictory to materialism. In reality it is the transfer of Feuerbach's materialistic doctrine. We may assert with certainty that Marx and Engels would have given attention to this trend of thought with the greatest interest."[104] This is a cautious assertion testifying that Marx and Engels in their writings never showed any interest in this trend of thought. Francè as a limited–minded naturalist knows only the antithesis of views in middle–class thinking; he assumes that materialists believe in matter only, hence the doctrine that in all matter there is something spiritual is, to him, no materialism at all. Plekhanov, on the other hand, considers it a small modification of materialism that makes it more resistant.

Lenin was quite well aware of the concordance of his views with middle–class materialism of the nineteenth century. For him "materialism" is the common basis of Marxism and middle–class materialism. After having expounded that Engels in his booklet on Feuerbach charged these materialists with three things,—that they remained with the materialist doctrine of the eighteenth century, that their materialism was mechanical, and that in the realm of social science, they held fast to idealism and did not understand Historical Materialism—he proceeds:

> Exclusively for these three things and exclusively within these limits, does Engels refute both the materialism of the eighteenth century and the doctrines of Büchner and Co.! On all other, more elementary, questions of materialism (questions distorted by the Machians) there is and can be no difference between Marx and Engels on the one hand and all these old materialists on the other.[105]

That this is an illusion of Lenin's has been demonstrated in the proceeding pages; these three things carry along as their consequences an utter difference in the fundamental epistemological ideas. And in the same way, Lenin continues, Engels was in accordance with Dühring in his materialism:

> For Engels . . . Dühring was not a sufficiently steadfast, clear and consistent materialist.[106]

Compare this with the way Engels finished Dühring off in words of scornful contempt.

Lenin's concordance with middle–class materialism and his ensuing discordance with Historical Materialism is manifest in many consequences. The former waged its main war against religion; and the chief reproach Lenin raises against Mach and his followers is that they sustain fideism. We met with it in several quotations already; in hundreds of places all through the book we find fideism as the opposite of materialism. Marx and Engels did not know of fideism; they drew the line between materialism and idealism. In the name fideism emphasis is laid upon religion. Lenin explains whence he took the word. "In France, those who put faith above reason are called fideists (from the Latin *fides*, faith)."[107]

This oppositeness of religion to reason is a reminiscence from pre–marxian times, from the emancipation of the middle–class, appealing to 'reason' in order to attack religious faith as the chief enemy in the social struggle; 'free thinking' was opposed to 'obscurantism.' Lenin, in continually pointing to fideism as the consequence of the contested doctrines indicates that also to him in the world of ideas religion is the chief enemy.

Thus he scolds Mach for saying that the problem of determinism cannot be settled empirically: in research, Mach says, every scientist must be determinist but in practical affairs he remains indeterminist.

> Is this not obscurantism . . . when determinism is confined to the field of 'investigation,' while in the field of morality, social activity, and all fields other than 'investigation' the question is left to a 'subjective' estimate . . . . And so things have been amicably divided: theory for the professors, practice for the theologians!"[108]

Thus every subject is seen from the point of view of religion. Manifestly it was unknown to Lenin that the deeply religious Calvinism was a rigidly deterministic doctrine, whereas the materialist middle–class of the nineteenth century put their faith into free will, hence proclaimed indeterminism. At this point a real Marxian thinker would not have missed the opportunity of explaining to the Russian Machists that it was Historical Materialism that opened the way for determinism in the field of society; we have shown above that the theoretical conviction that rules and laws hold in a realm—this means determinism—can find a foundation only when we succeed in establishing practically such laws and connections. Further, that Mach because he belonged to the middle class and was bound to its fundamental line of thought, by necessity was indeterminist in his social views; and that in this way his ideas were backward and incompatible with Marxism. But nothing of the sort is found in Lenin; that ideas are determined by class is not mentioned; the theoretical differences hang in the air. Of course theoretical ideas must be criticized by theoretical arguments. When, however, the social consequences are emphasized with such vehemence, the social origins of the contested ideas should not have been left out of consideration. This most essential character of Marxism does not seem to exist for Lenin.

So we are not astonished that among former authors it is especially Ernest Haeckel who is esteemed and praised by Lenin. In a final chapter inscribed "Ernst Haeckel and Ernst Mach" he compares and opposes them. "Mach . . . betrays science into the hands of fideism by virtually deserting to the camp of philosophical idealism."[109] But "every page" in Haeckel's work "is a slap in the face of the 'sacred' teachings of all official philosophy and theology." Haeckel "instantly, easily and simply revealed . . . that there is a foundation. This foundation is natural–scientific materialism."[110]

In his praise it does not disturb him that the writings of Haeckel combine, as generally recognized, popular science with a most superficial philosophy—Lenin himself speaks of his "philosophical naiveté" and says "that he does not enter into an investigation of philosophical fundamentals."[111] What is essential to him is that Haeckel was a dauntless fighter against prominent religious doctrines.

> The storm provoked by Ernst Haeckel's *The Riddle of the Universe* in every civilized country strikingly brought out, on the one hand, the partisan character of philosophy in modern society and, on the other, the true social significance of the struggle of materialism against idealism and agnosticism. The fact that the book was sold in hundreds of thousands of copies, that it was immediately translated into all languages and that it appeared in special cheap editions, clearly demonstrates that the book 'has found its way to the masses,' that there are numbers of readers whom Ernst Haeckel at once won over to his side. This popular little book became a weapon in the class struggle. The professors of philosophy and theology in every country of the world set about denouncing and annihilating Haeckel in every possible way.[112]

What class–fight was this? Which class was here represented by Haeckel against which other class! Lenin is silent on this point. Should his words be taken to imply that Haeckel, unwittingly, acted as a spokesman of the working class against the bourgeoisie? Then it must be remarked that Haeckel was a vehement opponent to socialism and that in his defense of Darwinism he tried to recommend it to the ruling class by pointing out that it was an aristocratic theory, the doctrine of the selection of the best, most fit to refute "the utter nonsense of socialist leveling."[113] What Lenin calls a tempest raised by the *Weltraetsel* was in reality only a breeze within the middle class, the last episode of its conversion from materialism to idealistic world conception. Haeckel's *Weltraetsel* was the last flare up, in a weakened form, of middle–class materialism, and the idealist, mystic, and religious tendencies were so strong already among the bourgeoisie and the intellectuals that from all sides they could pounce upon Haeckel's book and show up its deficiencies. What was the importance of the book for the mass of its readers among the working class we have indicated above. When Lenin speaks here of a class fight he demonstrates how little he knew of the class fight in countries of developed capitalism, and saw it only as a fight for and against religion.

Plekhanov's Views

The kinship with middle–class materialism revealed in Lenin's book is not simply a personal deviation from Marxism. Analogous views are found in Plekhanov, at the time the acknowledged first and prominent theorist of Russian socialism. In his book *Grundprobleme des Marxismus* (Fundamental Problems of Marxism), first written in Russian, with a German translation in 1910, he begins by broadly treating the concordance between Marx and Feuerbach. What usually is called Feuerbach's Humanism, he explains, means that Feuerbach proceeds from man to matter. "The words of Feuerbach quoted above on the 'human head' show that the question of 'brain matter' was answered at the time in a materialist sense. And this point of view was also accepted by Marx and Engels. It became the basis of their philosophy."[114] Of course Marx and Engels assumed that human thoughts are produced in the brain, just as they assumed that the earth revolved around the sun. Plekhanov, however, proceeds:

"When we deal with this thesis of Feuerbach, we get acquainted at the same time with the *philosophical side of Marxism.* " He then quotes the sentences of Feuerbach: "Thinking comes from being, but being comes not from thinking. Being exists in itself and by itself, existence has its basis in itself;" and he concludes by adding "Marx and Engels made this opinion on the relation between being and thinking the basis of their materialist conception of history."[115] Surely; but the question is what they mean by "being." In this colorless word many opposing concepts of later times are contained undistinguished. All that is perceptible to us we call being; from the side of natural science it can mean matter, from the side of social science the same word can mean the entire society. To Feuerbach it was the material substance of man: 'man is what he eats'; to Marx it is social reality, i.e., a society of people, tools, production–relations, that determines consciousness.

Plekhanov then speaks of the first of Marx's theses on Feuerbach; he says that Marx here "completes and deepens Feuerbach's ideas";[116] he explains that Feuerbach took man in his passive relations, Marx in his active relation to nature. He points to the later statement in *Das Kapital*: "Whilst man works upon outside nature and changes it, he changes at the same time his own nature," and he adds: "The profundity of this thought becomes clear in the light of Marx's theory of knowledge . . . . It must be admitted, though, that Marx's theory of knowledge is a direct offspring of Feuerbach's or, more rightly, represents Feuerbach's theory of knowledge which, then, has been deepened by Marx in a masterly way." And again, on the next page, he speaks of "modern materialism, the materialism of Feuerbach, Marx and Engels."[117] What must be admitted, rather, is that the ambiguous sentence 'being determines thought' is common to them, and that the materialist doctrine that brain produces thought is the most unessential part of Marxism and contains no trace yet of a real theory of knowledge.

The essential side of Marxism is what distinguished it from other materialist theories and what makes them the expression of different class struggles. Feuerbach's theory of knowledge, belonging to the fight for emancipation of the middle class, has its basis in the lack of science of society as the most powerful reality determining human thinking. Marxian theory of knowledge proceeds from the action of society, this self–made material world of man, upon the mind, and so belongs to the proletarian class struggle. Certainly Marx's theory of knowledge descended, historically, from Hegel and Feuerbach; but equally certainly it grew into something entirely different from Hegel and Feuerbach. It is a significant indication of the point of view of Plekhanov that he does not see this antagonism and that he assigns the main importance to the trivial community of opinion—which is unimportant for the real issue—that thoughts are produced by the brain.

The Russian Revolution

The concordance of Lenin and Plekhanov in their basic philo–sophical views and their common divergence from Marxism points to their common origin out of the Russian social con–ditions. The name and garb of a doctrine or theory depend on its spiritual descent; they indicate the earlier thinker to whom we feel most indebted and whom we think we follow. The real content, how–ever, depends on its material origin and is determined by the social conditions under which it developed and has to work. Marxism itself says that the main social ideas and spiritual trends express the aims of the classes, i.e., the needs of social development, and change with the class struggles themselves. So they cannot be understood isolated from society and class struggle. This holds for Marxism itself.

In their early days Marx and Engels stood in the first ranks of the middle–class opposition, not yet disjoined into its different social trends, against absolutism in Germany. Their development towards Historical Materialism, then, was the theoretical reflex of the devel–opment of the working class towards independent action against the bourgeoisie. The practical class–antagonism found its expression in the theoretical antagonism. The fight of the bourgeoisie against feu–dal dominance was expressed by middle–class materialism, cognate to Feuerbach's doctrine, which used natural science to fight religion as the consecration of the old powers. The working class in its own fight has little use for natural science, the instrument of its foe; its theoretical weapon is social science, the science of social develop–ment. To fight religion by means of natural science has no signifi–cance for the workers; they know, moreover, that its roots will be cut off anyhow first by capitalist development, then by their own class struggle. Neither have they any use for the obvious fact that thoughts are produced by the brain. They have to understand how ideas are produced by society. This is the content of Marxism, as it grows among the workers as a living and stirring power, as the theory expressing their growing power of organization and knowledge. When in the second half of the nineteenth century capitalism gained complete mastery in Western and Central Europe as well as in America, middle–class materialism disappeared. Marxism was the only materialist class–view remaining.

In Russia, however, matters were different. Here the fight against Czarism was analogous to the former fight against absolutism in Europe. In Russia too church and religion were the strongest supports of the system of government; they held the rural masses, engaged in primitive agrarian production, in complete ignorance and superstition. The struggle against religion was here a prime social necessity. Since in Russia there was no significant bourgeoisie that as a future ruling class could take up the fight, the task fell to the intelligentsia; during scores of years it waged a strenuous fight for enlightenment of the masses against Czarism. Among the Western bourgeoisie, now reactionary and anti–materialist, it could find no support whatever in this struggle. It had to appeal to the socialist workers, who alone sympathized with it, and it took over their acknowledged theory, Marxism. Thus it came about that even intellectuals who were spokesmen of the first rudiments of a Russian bourgeoisie, such as Peter Struve and Tugan–Baranovsky, presented themselves as Marxists.[118] They had nothing in common with the proletarian Marxism of the West; what they learned from Marx was the doctrine of social development with capitalism as the next phase. A power for revolution came up in Russia for the first time when the workers took up the fight, first by strikes only, then in combination with political demands. Now the intellectuals found a revolutionary class to join up with, in order to become its spokesmen in a socialist party.

Thus the proletarian class struggle in Russia was at the same time a struggle against Czarist absolutism, under the banner of socialism. So Marxism in Russia, developing as the theory of those engaged in the social conflict, necessarily assumed another character than in Western Europe. It was still the theory of a fighting working class; but this class had to fight first and foremost for what in Western

Europe had been the function and work of the bourgeoisie, with the intellectuals as its associates. So the Russian intellectuals, in adapting the theory to this local task, had to find a form of Marxism in which criticism of religion stood in the forefront. They found it in an approach to earlier forms of materialism, and in the first writings of Marx from the time when in Germany the fight of the bourgeoisie and the workers against absolutism was still undivided.

This appears most clearly in Plekhanov, the "father of Russian Marxism." At the time that in Western countries theorists occupied themselves with political problems, he turned his attention to the older materialists. In his *Beiträge zur Geschichte des Materialismus* (Contributions to the History of Materialism) he treats the French materialists of the eighteenth century, Helvetius, Lamettrie, and compares them with Marx, to show how many valuable and important ideas were already contained in their works.[119] Hence we understand why in his *Grundprobleme des Marxismus* he stresses the concordance between Marx and Feuerbach and emphasizes the viewpoints of middle–class materialism.

Yet Plekhanov was strongly influenced by the Western, especially the German, workers' movement. He was known as the herald of the Russian working–class struggle, which he predicted theoretically at a time when practically there was hardly any trace. He was esteemed as one of the very few who occupied themselves with philosophy; he played an international role and took part in the discussions on Marxism and reformism. Western socialists studied his writings without perceiving at the time the differences hidden within them. Thus he was determined by Russian conditions less exclusively than Lenin.

Lenin was the practical leader of the Russian revolutionary movement. Hence in his theoretical ideas its practical conditions and political aims are shown more clearly. The conditions of the fight against Czarism determined the basic views exposed in his book. Theoretical, especially philosophic views are not determined by abstract studies and chance reading in philosophical literature, but by the great life–tasks which, imposed by the needs of practical activity, direct the will and thought of man. To Lenin and the Bolshevik party the first life–task was the annihilation of Czarism and of the backward, barbarous social system of Russia. Church and religion were the theoretical foundations of that system, the ideology and glorification of absolutism, expression and symbol of the slavery of the masses. Hence a relentless fight against them was needed; the struggle against religion stood in the center of Lenin's theoretical thought; any concession however small to 'fideism' was an attack on the life–nerve of the movement. As a fight against absolutism, landed property, and clergy, the fight in Russia was very similar to the former fight of bourgeoisie and intellectuals in Western Europe; so the thoughts and fundamental ideas of Lenin must be similar to what had been propagated in middle–class materialism, and his sympathies went to its spokesmen. In Russia, however, it was the working class who had to wage the fight; so the fighting organization had to be a socialist party, proclaiming Marxism as its creed, and taking from Marxism what was necessary for the Russian Revolution: the doctrine of social development from capitalism to socialism, and the doctrine of class war as its moving force. Hence Lenin gave to his materialism the name and garb of Marxism, and assumed it to be the real—i.e., peculiarly working–class as contrasted with middle–class—Marxism.

This identification was supported by still another circumstance. In Russia capitalism had not grown up gradually from small–scale production in the hands of a middle class, as it had in Western Europe. Big industry was imported from outside as a foreign element by Western capitalism exploiting the Russian workers. Moreover Western financial capital, by its loans to Czarism, exploited the entire agrarian Russian people, who were heavily taxed to pay the interests. Western capital here assumed the character of colonial capital, with the Czar and his officials as its agents. In countries exploited as colonies all the classes have a common interest in throwing off the yoke of the usurious foreign capital, to establish their own free economic development, leading as a rule to home capitalism. This fight is waged against world–capital, hence often under the name of socialism; and the workers of the Western countries, who stand against the same foe, are the natural allies. Thus in China Sun Yat–sen was a socialist; since, however, the Chinese bourgeoisie whose spokesman he was, was a numerous and powerful class, his socialism was 'national' and he opposed the 'errors' of Marxism.

Lenin, on the contrary, had to rely on the working class, and because his fight had to be implacable and radical, he espoused the
most radical ideology of the Western proletariat fighting world–capitalism, viz. Marxism. Since, however, the Russian revolution showed
a mixture of two characters, middle–class revolution in its immediate aims, proletarian revolution in its active forces, the appropriate
Bolshevik theory too had to present two characters, middle–class
materialism in its basic philosophy, proletarian evolutionism in its
doctrine of class fight. This mixture was termed Marxism. But it is
clear that Lenin's Marxism, as determined by the special Russian attitude toward capitalism, must be fundamentally different from the
real Marxism growing as their basic view in the workers of the countries of big capitalism. Marxism in Western Europe is the worldview
of a working class confronting the task of converting a most highly
developed capitalism, its own world of life and action, into communism. The Russian workers and intellectuals could not make this their
object; they had first to open the way for a free development of a
modern industrial society.[C] To the Russian marxists the nucleus of
Marxism is not contained in Marx's thesis that social reality determines consciousness, but in the sentence of young Marx, inscribed
in big letters in the Moscow People's House, that religion is the opium
of the people.

It may happen that in a theoretical work there appear not the immediate surroundings and tasks of the author, but more general and
remote influences and wider tasks. In Lenin's book, however, nothing of the sort is perceptible. It is a manifest and exclusive reflection
of the Russian Revolution at which he was aiming. Its character so
entirely corresponds to middle–class materialism that, if it had been
known at the time in Western Europe—but only confused rumors
on the internal strifes of Russian socialism penetrated here—and if it
could have been rightly interpreted, one could have predicted that
the Russian revolution must somehow result in a kind of capitalism
based on a workers' struggle.

There is a widespread opinion that the Bolshevik party was Marxist, and that it was only for practical reasons that Lenin, the great
scholar and leader of Marxism, gave to the revolution another direction than what Western workers called communism—thereby show-

ing his realistic marxian insight. The critical opposition to the Russian and C[ommunist] P[arty] politics tries indeed to oppose the despotic practice of the present Russian government—termed Stalinism—to the 'true' Marxist principles of Lenin and old Bolshevism. Wrongly so. Not only because in practice these polities were inaugurated already by Lenin. But also because the alleged Marxism of Lenin and the Bolshevik party is nothing but a legend. Lenin never knew real Marxism. Whence should he have taken it? Capitalism he knew only as colonial capitalism; social revolution he knew only as the annihilation of big land ownership and Czarist despotism. Russian bolshevism cannot be reproached for having abandoned the way of Marxism; for it was never on that way. Every page of Lenin's philosophical work is there to prove it; and Marxism itself, by its thesis that theoretical opinions are determined by social relations and necessities, makes clear that it could not be otherwise. Marxism, however, at the same time shows the necessity of the legend; every middle–class revolution, requiring working class and peasant support, needs the illusion that it is something different, larger, more universal. Here it was the illusion that the Russian revolution was the first step of world revolution liberating the entire proletarian class from capitalism; its theoretical expression was the legend of Marxism.

Of course Lenin was a pupil of Marx; from Marx he had learnt what was most essential for the Russian revolution, the uncompromising proletarian class struggle. Just as for analogous reasons, the social–democrats were pupils of Marx. And surely the fight of the Russian workers, in their mass actions and their soviets, was the most important practical example of modern proletarian warfare. That, however, Lenin did not understand Marxism as the theory of proletarian revolution, that he did not understand capitalism, bourgeoisie, proletariat in their highest modern development, was shown strikingly when from Russia, by means of the Third International, the world revolution was to be started, and the advice and warnings of Western Marxists were entirely disregarded. An unbroken series of blunders, failures, and defeats, of which the present weakness of the workers' movement was the result, showed the unavoidable shortcoming of the Russian leadership.

Returning now to the time that Lenin wrote his book we have to ask what then was the significance of the controversy on Machism. The Russian revolutionary movement comprised wider circles of intellectuals than Western socialism; so part of them came under the influence of anti–materialist middle–class trends. It was natural that Lenin should sharply take up the fight against such tendencies. He did not look upon them as would a Marxist who understands them as a social phenomenon, explaining them out of their social origin, and thus rendering them ineffectual; nowhere in his book do we find an attempt at or a trace of such an understanding. To Lenin materialism was the truth established by Feuerbach, Marx and Engels, and the middle–class materialists; but then stupidity, reaction, money–interests of the bourgeoisie, and the spiritual power of theology had brought about a revulsion in Europe. Now this corruption threatened to assail bolshevism too; so it had to be opposed with the utmost vigor.

In this action Lenin of course was entirely right. To be sure, it was not a question of the truth of Marx or Mach, nor whether out of Mach's ideas something could be used in Marxism. It was the question whether middle–class materialism or middle–class idealism, or some mixture, would afford the theoretical basis for the fight against Czarism. It is clear that the ideology of a self–contented, already declining bourgeoisie can never fit in with a rising movement, not even with a rising middle–class itself. It would have led to weakness, where unfolding of the utmost vigor was necessary. Only the rigor of materialism could make the Party hard, such as was needed for a revolution. The tendency of Machism, somehow parallel to revisionism in Germany, was to break the radicalism of struggle and the solid unity of the party, in theory and in practice. This was the danger that Lenin saw quite clearly. "When I read it (Bogdanov's book) I became exceedingly provoked and enraged," he wrote to Gorky, February 1908.[120] Indeed, we perceive this in the vehemence of his attack upon the adversary, in every page of the work; it seems to have been written in a continuous fury. It is not a fundamental discussion clearing the ideas, as was, for example Engels' book against Dühring; it is the war–pamphlet of a party leader who has to ward off by any means the danger to his party. So it could not be expected that he should try really to understand the hostile doctrines; in consequence of his own unmarxian thinking he could only misinterpret and misrepresent them. The only thing needed was to knock them down, to destroy their scientific credit, and thus to expose the Russian Machists as ignorant parrots of reactionary blockheads.

And he succeeded. His fundamental views were the views of the Bolshevik party at large, as determined by its historical task. As so often, Lenin had felt exactly the practical exigencies. Machism was condemned and expelled from the party. As a united body the party could take its course again, in the van of the working class, towards the revolution.

The words of Deborin quoted in the beginning thus are only partially true. We cannot speak of a victory of Marxism, when there is only question of a so–called refutation of middle–class idealism through the ideas of middle–class materialism. But doubtless Lenin's book was an important feature in the history of the Party, determining in a high degree the further development of philosophic opinions in Russia. Hereafter the revolution, under the new system of state capitalism—a combination of middle–class materialism and the marxian doctrine of social development, adorned with some dialectical terminology—was, under the name 'Leninism', proclaimed the official State–philosophy. It was the right doctrine for the Russian intellectuals who, now that natural science and technics formed the basis of a rapidly developing production system under their direction, saw the future open up before them as the ruling class of an immense empire.

The Proletarian Revolution

The publication first of a German, then of an English translation of Lenin's work shows that it was meant to play a wider role than its function in the old Russian party conflict. It is presented now to the younger generation of socialists and communists in order to influence the international workers' movement. So we ask: what can the workers in capitalist countries learn from it? Of the refuted philosophical ideas it gives a distorted view; and under the name of Marxism another theory, middle–class materialism is expounded. It does not aim at bringing the reader to a clear independent judgment in philosophical questions; it intends to instruct him that the Party is right, and that he has to trust and to follow the party leaders. What way is it that this party leader shows to the international proletariat? Let us read Lenin's view of the world–contest of the classes in his final sentences: ". . . behind the epistemological scholasticism of empirio–criticism it is impossible not to see the struggle of parties in philosophy, a struggle which in the last analysis reflects the tendencies and ideology of the antagonistic classes in modern society . . . . The contending parties are essentially . . . materialism and idealism. The latter is merely a subtle, refined form of fideism, which stands fully armed, commands vast organizations and steadily continues to exercise influence on the masses, turning the slightest vacillation in philosophical thought to its own advantage. The objective class role played by empirio–criticism entirely consists in rendering faithful service to the fideists in their struggle against materialism in general and historical materialism in particular."[121]

Nothing here of the immense power of the foe, the bourgeoisie, master of all the riches of the world, against which the working class hardly can make any progress. Nothing of its spiritual power over the minds of the workers, still strongly dominated by middle–class culture and hardly able to overcome it in a continuous struggle for knowledge. Nothing of the new powerful ideologies of nationalism and imperialism threatening to gain a hold over the workers too, and indeed, soon afterwards, dragging them along into the world war. No, the Church, the organization of 'fideism' in full armor, that is to Lenin the most dangerous hostile power. The fight of materialism against religious belief is to him the theoretical fight accompanying the class struggle. The limited theoretical opposition between the former and the later ruling class appears to him the great world fight of ideas which he connects with the proletarian class fight, the essence and ideas of which lie far outside his view. Thus in Lenin's philosophy the Russian scheme is transferred upon Western Europe and America, the anti–religious tendency of a rising bourgeoisie is transferred to the rise of the proletariat. Just as among German reformists at that time the division was made between 'reaction' and 'progress' and not according to class but according to political ideology—thus confusing the workers—so here it is made according to religious ideology, between reactionaries and free–thinkers. Instead of establishing its class–unity against bourgeoisie and State, to get mastery over production, the Western proletarian class is invited to take up the fight against religion. If this book and these ideas of Lenin had been known in 1918 among Western Marxists, surely there would have been a more critical attitude against his tactics for world revolution.

The Third International aims at a world revolution after the model of the Russian revolution and with the same goal. The Russian economic system is state capitalism, there called state–socialism or even communism, with production directed by a state bureaucracy under the leadership of the Communist Party. The state officials, forming the new ruling class, have the disposal over the product, hence over the surplus value, whereas the workers receive wages only, thus forming an exploited class. In this way it has been possible in the short time of some dozens of years to transform Russia from a primitive barbarous country into a modern state of rapidly increasing industry on the basis of advanced science and technics. According to Communist Party ideas, a similar revolution is needed in the capitalist countries, with the working class again as the active power, leading to the overthrow of the bourgeoisie and the organization of production by a state bureaucracy. The Russian revolution could be victorious only because a well–disciplined, united Bolshevik party led the masses, and because in the party the clear insight and the unyielding assurance of Lenin and his friends showed the right way. Thus, in the same way, in world revolution the workers have to follow the Communist Party, leave to it the lead and afterwards the government; and the party members have to obey their leaders in rigid discipline. Essential are the qualified capable party leaders, the proficient, experienced revolutionaries; what is necessary for the masses is the belief that the party and its leaders are right.

In reality, for the working class in the countries of developed capitalism, in Western Europe and America, matters are entirely different. Its task is not the overthrow of a backward absolutist monarchy. Its task is to vanquish a ruling class commanding the mightiest material and spiritual forces the world ever knew. Its object cannot be to replace the domination of stockjobbers and monopolists over a disorderly production by the domination of state officials over a production regulated from above. Its object is to be itself master of production and itself to regulate labor, the basis of life. Only then is capitalism really destroyed. Such an aim cannot be attained by an ignorant mass, confident followers of a party presenting itself as an expert leadership. It can be attained only if the workers themselves, the entire class, understand the conditions, ways and means of their fight; when every man knows from his own judgment what to do. They must, every man of them, act themselves, decide themselves, hence think out and know for themselves. Only in this way will a real class organization be built up from below, having the form of something like workers' councils. It is of no avail that they have been convinced that their leaders know what is afoot and have gained the point in theoretical discussion—an easy thing when each is acquainted with the writings of his own party only. Out of the contest of arguments they have to form a clear opinion themselves. There is no truth lying ready at hand that has only to be imbibed; in every new case truth must be contrived by exertion of one's own brain.

This does not mean, of course, that every worker should judge on scientific arguments in fields that can be mastered only by professional study. It means, first, that all workers should give attention not only to their direct working and living conditions but also to the great social issues connected with their class struggle and the organization of labor; and should know how to take decisions here. But it implies, secondly, a certain standard of argument in propaganda and political strife. When the views of the opponent are rendered in a distorted way because the willingness or the capacity to understand them is lacking, then in the eyes of the believing adherents you may score a success; but the only result—intended indeed in party strife— is to bind them with stronger fanaticism to the party. For the workers however, what is of importance is not the increase of power of a party but the increase of their own capacity to seize power and to establish their mastery over society. Only when, in arguing and discussing, the opponent is given his full pound, when in weighing arguments against one another each solid opinion is understood out of social class relations, will the participant hearers gain such well founded insight as is necessary for a working class to assure its freedom.

The working class needs Marxism for its liberation. Just as the results of natural science are necessary for the technical construction of capitalism, so the results of social science are necessary for the organizational construction of communism. What was needed first was political economy, that part of Marxism that expounds the structure of capitalism, the nature of exploitation, the class–antagonism, the tendencies of economic development. It gave, directly, a solid basis to the spontaneously arising fight of the workers against the capitalist masters. Then, in the further struggle, by its theory of the development of society from primitive economy through capitalism to communism, it gave confidence and enthusiasm through the prospect of victory and freedom. When the not yet numerous workers took up their first difficult fight, and the hopeless indifferent masses had to be roused, this insight was the first thing needed.

When the working class has grown more numerous, more powerful, and society is full of the proletarian class struggle, another part of Marxism has to come to the forefront. That they should know that they are exploited and have to fight, is not the main point any more; they must know how to fight, how to overcome their weakness, how to build up their unity and strength. Their economic position is so easy to understand, their exploitation so manifest that their unity in struggle, their common will to seize power over production should presumably result at once. What hampers them is chiefly the power of the inherited and infused ideas, the formidable spiritual power of the middle–class world, enveloping their minds into a thick cloud of beliefs and ideologies, dividing them, and making them uncertain and confused. The process of enlightenment, of clearing up and vanquishing this world of old ideas and ideologies is the essential process of building the working–class power, is the progress of revolution. Here that part of Marxism is needed that we call its philosophy, the relation of ideas to reality.

Among these ideologies the least significant is religion. As the withered husk of a system of ideas reflecting conditions of a far past, it has only an imaginary power as a refuge for all, who are frightened by capitalist development. Its basis has been continually undermined by capitalism itself. Middle–class philosophy then put up in its place the belief in all those lesser idols, deified abstractions, such as matter, force, causality in nature, liberty, and progress in society. In modern times these now forsaken idols have been replaced by new, more powerful objects of veneration: state and nation. In the struggle of the old and the new bourgeoisies for world power, nationalism, now the most needed ideology, rose to such power as to carry with it even broad masses of the workers. Most important are, besides, such spiritual powers as democracy, organization, union, party, because they have their roots in the working class itself as results of their life practice, their own struggle. Just because there is connected with them the remembrance of passionate exertion, of devoted sacrifices, of feverish concern with victory or defeat, their merit—which is bound as a class tool to those particular past times and conditions—is exalted to the belief in their absolute excellence. That makes the transition to new necessities under new conditions difficult. The conditions of life frequently compel the workers to take up new forms of fight; but the old traditions can hamper and retard it in a serious way. In the continuous contest between inherited ideology and practical needs, it is essential for the workers to understand that their ideas are not independently existing truths but generalizations of former experiences and necessities; that human mind always has the tendency to assign to such ideas an unlimited validity, as absolutely good or bad, venerated or hated, and thus makes the people slaves to superstition; but that by understanding limits and conditions, super-stition is vanquished and thought is made free. And, conversely, what is recognized as the lasting interest, as the essential basis of the fight for his class, must be unerringly kept in mind—though without be-ing deified—as the brilliant guiding star in all action. This—besides its use as explanation of daily experience and class struggle—is the significance of Marxian philosophy, the doctrine of the connection of world and mind, as conceived by Marx, Engels, and Dietzgen; this gives strength to the working class to accomplish its great task of self–liberation.

Lenin's book, on the other hand, tries to impose upon the readers the author's belief in the reality of abstractions. So it cannot be help-ful in any way for the workers' task. And as a matter of fact its publi-cation in Western languages was not meant to be that. Workers aim-ing at the self–liberation of their class stand beyond the horizon of the Communist Party. What the Communist Party can see is the competitor, the rival party, the Second International trying to keep the leadership over the working class. As Deborin was quoted in the Preface, the aim of the publication was to win social–democracy, cor-rupted by middle–class idealistic philosophy, back to materialism—or else to browbeat it by the more captivating radical terms of mate-rialism—as a theoretical contribution to the Red Front. For the ris-ing class–movement of the workers it matters little which of these unmarxian party lines of thought should get the upper hand.

But in another way Lenin's philosophy may be of importance for their struggle. The aim of the Communist Party—which it called world–revolution—is to bring to power, by means of the fighting force of the workers, a layer of leaders who then establish planned production by means of State–Power; in its essence it coincides with the aims of social democracy. The social ideals growing up in the minds of the intellectual class now that it feels its increasing impor-tance in the process of production—a well–ordered organization of production for use under the direction of technical and scientific experts are hardly different. So the Communist Party considers this class its natural allies which it has to draw into its circle. By an able theoretical propaganda it tries to detach the intelligentsia from the spiritual influences of the declining bourgeoisie and of private capitalism, and to win them for the revolution that will put them into their proper place as a new leading and ruling class. Or, in philosophical terms, to win them for materialism. A revolution cannot be made with the meek, softening ideology of a system of idealism, but only under the inspiring daring radicalism of materialist thought. For this the foundation is afforded by Lenin's book. On this basis an extensive literature of articles, reviews, and books has already been published, first in German and then in still greater numbers in English, in Europe and in America, with the collaboration of well–known Russian scholars and Western scientists sympathizing with the Communist Party. The contents of these writings make clear at first sight that they are not destined for the working class but for the intellectuals of these countries. Leninism is here expounded before them— under the name of Marxism, or 'dialectics'—and they are told that it is the fundamental all–embracing world–doctrine, in which the special sciences must be seen as subordinate parts. It is clear that with real Marxism, as the theory of the real proletarian revolution, such propaganda would have no chance; but with Leninism, as a theory of middle–class revolution installing a new ruling class, it might be successful.

There is of course this difficulty, that the intellectual class is too limited in number, too heterogeneous in social position, hence too feeble to be able single–handed to seriously threaten capitalist domination. Neither are the leaders of the Second and the Third International a match for the power of the bourgeoisie, even if they could impose themselves by strong and clear politics instead of being rotten through opportunism. When, however, capitalism is tumbling into a heavy economic or political crisis which rouses the masses, when the working class has taken up the fight and succeeds in shattering capitalism in a first victory—then their time will come. Then they will intervene and slide themselves in as leaders of the revolution nominally to give their aid by taking part in the fight, in reality to deflect the action in the direction of their party aims. Whether or not the beaten bourgeoisie will then rally with them to save of capitalism what can be saved, in any case their intervention comes down to cheating the workers, leading them off from the road to freedom.

Here we see the possible significance of Lenin's book for the future working class movement. The Communist Party, though it may lose ground among the workers, tries to form with the socialists and the intellectual class a united front, ready at the first major crisis of capitalism to take in its hands the power over and against the workers. Leninism and its philosophical textbook then will serve, under the name of Marxism, to overawe the workers and to impose upon the intellectuals, as the leading system of thought by which the reactionary spiritual powers are beaten. Thus the fighting working class, basing itself upon Marxism, will find Lenin's philosophical work a stumbling block in its way, as the theory of a class that tries to perpetuate its serfdom.

Pannekoek's Notes

^AThese obsolete ideas as an essential part of Leninism as the Russian State–philosophy, were afterwards imposed upon Russian science, as may be inferred from the following communication in Waldemar Kaempfert's *Science in Soviet Russia*: "Toward the end of the Trotsky purge, the Astronomical Division of the Academy of Sciences passed some impassioned resolutions, which were signed by the president and eighteen members and which declared that 'modern bourgeois cosmogony is in a state of deep ideological confusion resulting from its refusal to accept the only true dialectical–materialistic concept, namely the infinity of the universe with respect to space as well as time,' a belief in relativity was branded as 'counter–revolutionary.'" [Reference unknown. Waldemar Kampfert (1877–1956)—interestingly, the cousin of logical positivist and Marxist philosopher Otto Neurath—was science editor of the *New York Times* for much of his career.—Editor]

^BDiderot, one of the Encyclopaedists of the eighteenth century, had written "that the faculty of sensation is a general property of matter, or a product of its organization." The wider scope admitted in the latter expression was dropped by Lenin. [Denis Diderot (1713–1784), from his "Conversation between Diderot and D'Alambert," in *Diderot: Interpreter of Nature: Selected Writings*, ed. Jonathan Kemp (New York: International Publishers, 1943), 49.—Editor]

^CBolshevik historians, since they know capitalism only in the character of colonial capitalism, were keen in recognizing the role of colonial capital in the world, and were able to write excellent studies on it. But at the same time they readly overlooked its differences from home capitalism. Thus Pokrovskii in his *History of Russia* represents 1917 as the end of a capitalist development of many centuries. [Mikhail Nikolaevich Pokrovskii (1868–1932), famed Russian historian, was author of *A History of Russia, from the Earliest Times to the Rise of Commercial Capitalism*, new introduction by Jesse D. Clarkson, trans. and ed. by J. D. Clarkson and M. D. M. Griffiths (Bloomington, IN: University Prints and Reprints, 1966) —Editor]

About the Editor's Notes: Pannekoek's citation and translation of other authors is occasionally loose and frequently obscure (both textually and historically) to modern readers. As a compromise between competing obligations to Pannekoek, the authors he cites, and the intended reader of this edition, in the body of the text I have retained Pannekoek's translations while providing page and volume references to more critically reliable and readily available editions in the Editor's notes. To maximize the usefulness of this edition for English readers, whenever possible, standard English translations have been cited; when no translation exists, the best German edition of the text is cited. All numbered notes below are the editor's and are intended to provide only historical, biographical, and bibliographical information, not a commentary on the text itself. In addition to the notes given below, there are three Editor's notes appended to Pannekoek's lettered notes (A, B, and C, on p. 163).

Editor's Notes

[1] The split between the Bolsheviks (in Russian: Majoritarians) and Mensheviks (in Russian: Minoritarians) in the Russian Social Democrat Labor Party occurred over membership requirements for the party at the Second Party Congress in 1903. The Bolsheviks, under V. I. Lenin (1870–1924), demanded active participation in official party organs as a condition for membership, while the Mensheviks, under Y. O. Martov (1873–1923) and Paul Axelrod (1850–1928), favored less stringent requirements. These divisions widened following the Revolution of 1905 until the establishment of a separate Menshevik party in 1912 (the Russian Social Democratic Labor Party) which rejected Leninist political strategy and tactics. After the October Revolution in 1917, which they considered an illegitimate *coup d'état*, the Mensheviks alternately supported and opposed the Bolsheviks during the Civil War until their suppression (along with all non–Bolshevik parties) following the Kronstadt Revolt in 1921. See *The Mensheviks in the Russian Revolution*, Abraham Ascher, ed. (Ithaca, N.Y.: Cornell University Press, 1976).

[2] The 'Austrian School', or Austro–Marxism, arose in Vienna around the turn of the century and included among its better known members Otto Bauer (1881–1938), Karl Renner (1870–1950), and Rudolf Hilferding (1877–1941). Austro–Marxism strongly resisted the revisionism of the Second International and defended the work of Marx as truly scientific and not merely political in its

importance. Their efforts to relate Marxist thought to the developing science of sociology and to the then–prominent positivist and Neo–Kantian elements in philosophy, as well as the broad range of cultural and scientific problems on which they worked, make them important precursors to the Frankfurt School. Renner in particular is an important figure within the Council communism movement. See *Austro–Marxism*, Tom Bottomore and Patrick Goode, eds. and trans. (Oxford: Oxford University Press, 1978), especially the introduction.

The 'Dutch School' refers to the Council communism espoused by Pannekoek, Herman Gorter (1864–1927), and Henriette Roland–Holst (1869–1952) inter alia from the first decade of the twentieth century onwards. They vigorously opposed the gradualism and reformism of the Second International as well as the Third International's strategy of forming parliamentary coalitions with bourgeois parties, preferring extra–legal mass action by the Proletariat aimed at undermining the social foundations of the capitalist system. For a fuller discussion of the history and ideas of Council communism, see *Pannekoek and Gorter's Marxism*, D. A. Smart, ed. (London: Pluto, 1978); John Gerber, "The Formation of Pannekoek's Marxism," in Serge Bricianer, ed., *Pannekoek and the Worker's Councils* (St. Louis: Telos, 1978), 1–30.

[3]V. I. Lenin, *State and Revolution*, in *Collected Works*, 45 vols. (Moscow: Progress Publishers, 1960–70; hereafter cited as *CW*), 25:385–498, especially 488–496. All subsequent references to texts by Lenin are to this edition; the first reference to a work will include volume and pagination for the entire text, while all subsequent references are to specific pages only. Pannekoek garnered Lenin's praise in *State and Revolution* for criticizing the willingness of Karl Kautsky (1854–1923) to participate in parliamentary bodies, only to be excoriated three years later in *Left–Wing Commuism: An Infantile Disorder* (*CW* 31:17–117) for his own refusal to do so.

[4]This "increasing opposition" was mere wishful thinking by Pannekoek. Council communism, which met only very limited success during the heyday of social unrest following the First World War, was quickly overshadowed by the Leninist model installed in the Soviet Union. By 1938, when Pannekoek wrote, it was completely moribund.

[5]*CW* 14:17–361.

[6]Ernst Mach (1838–1916), a leading Austrian physicist, was the first major thinker to reject Newton's belief in the absolute nature of space and time. As such, he was an important predecessor to Einstein's theory of relativity, as well as an accomplished physicist in his own right. For a brief but sound overview of his positions and their implications for Marxist theory at the turn of the century, see Robert C. Williams, *Lenin and His Critics, 1904–1914* (Bloomington, IN: Indiana University Press, 1986), especially chapters 2 and 7.

[7]Alexander Bogdanov (1873–1928), scientist, novelist, and revolutionary, was the first to attempt to integrate Mach's thought into Marxist philosophy. These efforts, combined with his greater political moderation, led to Lenin's engineering of his ouster from the Bolshevik leadership in 1909 and subsequent demonization within Soviet Marxism. Recently, in the post–Soviet era, there has been a renewed interest in his thought; see David G. Rowley, "Bogdanov and Lenin: Epistemology and Revolution," *Studies in East European Thought* 48 (1996): 1–19. Anatoli Luncharsky (1875–1933), despite his early association with Bogdanov, played an

important role in both the 1917 Revolution and the Soviet Government, serving as Commisar of Education from 1917 until 1929. He was awaiting appointment as ambassador to Spain when he died.

[8]Georgi Plekhanov (1857–1918) was the leading figure within Russian Marxism prior to Lenin, despite his self–imposed exile in Switzerland from 1880 onward. Although a Menshevik after 1903, he opposed Machism and his influence on Lenin was considerable, as evidenced by his reputation within Soviet philosophy after his death.

[9]Deborin, or Abram Ioffe (1881–1963), became one of the most prominent Soviet philosophers of the late 1920s for his support of dialectical materialism against the mechanistic materialism of I. I. Stepanov (1870–1928) and his insistence that the dialectic be employed as "a method of discovery, which should guide our scientific inquiries" (Gustav A. Wetter, *Dialectical Materialism: A Historical and Systematic Survey of Philosophy in the Soviet Union*, trans. Peter Heath [New York: Frederick A. Praeger, 1958], 131–32). He was stripped of power by Stalin in the early 1930s. The text referred to by Pannekoek may be found in the earliest English edition of Lenin's *Materialism and Empirio–Criticism* (New York: International Publishers, 1927), xxi–xxii.

[10]The classic—if at times misleading—statement of the relationship of Karl Marx (1818–1883) and Frederick Engels (1820–1895) to Hegelianism is Engels' *Ludwig Feuerbach and the End of Classical German Philosophy*, in Karl Marx and Frederick Engels, *Collected Works*, 50 vols. (New York: International Publishers, 1975– ; hereafter cited as *MECW*), 26:357–98. All page references to Marx's text are to this edition; as with Lenin's writings, the first reference to a text gives its volume and full pagination while all subsequent references are to specific page numbers. Over the last forty years, the 'Young Hegelians' have been the focus of extensive research, both in their own right and in their relationship to the work of the young Marx. See especially *The Young Hegelians: An Anthology*, Lawrence S. Stepelevich, ed. (Cambridge: Cambridge University Press, 1983); David McLellan, *The Young Hegelians and Karl Marx* (London: MacMillan, 1969); John Toews, *Hegelianism* (Cambridge: Cambridge University Press, 1980), especially 203–369. For a fresh perspective on Marx's philosophical thought during this formative period, see Daniel Brudney, *Marx's Attempt to Leave Philosophy* (Cambridge, Mass.: Harvard University Press, 1998).

[11]Karl Marx, "Difference between the Democritean and Epicurean Philosophy of Nature," *MECW* 1:25–108.

[12]For a more detailed discussion of the philosophy of Ludwig Feuerbach (1804–1872), see Marx W. Wartofsky, *Feuerbach* (Cambridge: Cambridge University Press, 1977); Van A. Harvey, *Feuerbach and the Interpretation of Religion* (Cambridge: Cambridge University Press, 1997).

[13]Engels, *Ludwig Feuerbach*, *MECW* 26:364: "Then came Feuerbach's *Wesen des Christenthums*. With one blow it pulverised the contradiction [between idea and reality], by plainly placing materialism on the throne again . . . . The spell was broken; the 'system' [of Hegel] was exploded and cast aside, and the contradictions shown to exist only in our imagination, was dissolved.—One must have experienced the liberating effect of this book for oneself to get an idea of it. Enthusiasm was universal: we were all Feuerbachians for a moment."

[14]Karl Marx, *Critique of the Hegelian Philosophy of Right, MECW* 3:175–87, 175–76.

[15] *The Poverty of Philosophy, MECW* 6:105–212; Karl Marx and Frederick Engels, *Communist Manifesto, MECW* 6:477–519; Karl Marx, "Preface" to *Outlines of the Critique of Political Economy, MECW* 28:17–48.

[16] *MECW* 26:365–366. Pannekoek's other reference is to Frederick Engels, *Anti–Dühring, MECW 25:1–309.*

[17] Marx, *Theses on Feuerbach, MECW* 5:6–8, 7.

[18] Marx and Engels, *The German Ideology, MECW* 5:19–539.

[19] David Borisovich Goldenach, or Ryazonov (1870–1938), was the founder as well as the chief of the Marx–Engels Institute in Moscow until his removal and eventual imprisonment under Stalin in 1930.

[20] *MECW* 5:36.

[21] *MECW* 5:41.

[22] *MECW* 5:37.

[23] 'Epistemology', the English translation of *Erkenntniskritik*, lacks entirely this critical connotation.

[24] *MECW* 5:6–7.

[25] *MECW* 26:368. Engel's example of alizarin was also used several times by Lenin in *Materialism and Empirio–Criticism.*

[26] Pannekoek's line of thought in this rather dense paragraph seems to be: Materialism, like any metaphysical doctrine, is not subject to proof by scientific experiment. Rather, it is the necessary presupposition of all truly scientific explanations of events in the world since only materialism posits a universe in which all its constituents are capable of producing sense impressions (a feature unique to material objects) and thus becoming possible objects of human knowledge. On the other hand, the transcendent and unknowable 'Thing–in–itself', by Kant's own admission, was posited not for scientific but for moral and religious reasons: "Even the assumption—as made on behalf of the necessary practical employment of my reason—of God, freedom, and immortality is not permissible unless at the same time speculative reason be deprived of its pretensions to transcendent insight . . . . I have therefore found it necessary to deny knowledge, in order to make room for faith" (Immanuel Kant, *Critique of Pure Reason*, trans. Norman Kemp Smith [New York: St. Martin's Press, 1965], Bxxx). Since the justification for positing the 'Thing–in–itself' lies not in science but in religion and morality, it is necessary only to account for the content of these in terms of historical materialism in order to remove the need for any intrinsically unknowable aspect of nature. Absent the Kantian 'Thing–in–itself', matter can safely be considered the ultimate foundation of the world.

[27] Karl Marx, *Capital, MECW* 35–37.

[28] *MECW* 5:8.

[29] Jacob Moleschott (1822–1893), a leading nineteenth century physiologist, argued for a purely physical account of all aspects of the human person, including consciousness and the emotions. Karl Vogt (1817–1895), exiled German scientist and the subject of Marx's scathing *Herr Vogt* (*MECW* 17:21–329), argued for a materialist account of consciousness and denied the existence of an immortal soul. Ludwig Büchner (1824–1899), author of the highly influential *Kraft und Stoff: Empirisch–naturphilosophische Studien* (Leipzig: T. Thomas, 1855), was perhaps the leading exponent in the late nineteenth century of reductivist and mechanistic

materialism. All three thinkers are mentioned by Engels in his *Ludwig Feuerbach* (*MECW* 26:369), upon which both Pannekoek and Lenin are heavily dependent.

[30]Ernst Haeckel (1834–1919), German physician and scientist, was the first and most energetic advocate of Darwinism in Germany. His widely read *The Riddle of the Universe at the close of the Nineteenth Century*, trans. Joseph McCabe (Grosse Point, Mich.: Scholarly Press, 1968), argued for a form of evolutionary pan-psychism which denied both the immortality of the soul and human freedom.

[31]The truth of Pannekoek's observation here can be shown by the divide throughout most of the twentieth century between the concern among English and American philosophers (who have been little influenced by Marx) with the philosophy of mind and the ontology of consciousness, and the Continental preoccupation with subjectivity and the conditions of its constitution.

[32]Pannekoek's description of the career of Joseph Dietzgen (1828–1888) is accurate, although the assessment of his philosophical ability and importance is greatly exaggerated. Dietzgen's most notable contribution to Marxist philosophy is his introduction of the term 'dialectical materialism.' His most important writings can be found in English translation in *The Positive Outcome of Philosophy*, trans. Ernest Untermann; introduction by Anton Pannekoek (Chicago: C. H. Kerr, 1928), and *Some of the Philosophical Essays on Socialism and Science, Religion, Ethics, Critique–of–Reason, and the World–at–large*, trans. M. Beer and Th. Rothstein (Chicago: C. H. Kerr, 1906).

[33]The reference here is unclear. Lenin wrote of him that, "in that worker–philosopher, who discovered dialectical materialism in his own way, there is much that is great!" (*CW* 14:247) Furthermore, Eugene Dietzgen, his son, reports that "At the international congress at The Hague, in 1872, to which my father was a delegate, Karl Marx introduced him to the assembled delegates, with the words: 'Here is our philosopher.'" (Dietzgen, *Positive Outcome*, 15), but there is no reference to this in Marx's address "On the Hague Conference of September 8, 1872" (*MECW* 23:256–58). Most likely, Pannekoek has conflated the views of Marx and Engels with those of Herman Gorter, who refers to Dietzgen as "*der Philosoph des Proletariats*" in his *Der historische Materialismus für Arbeiter erklärt*, dritte bedeutend vermehrte ausgabe (Berlin: Buchhandlung für arbeiterliteratur, 1928), 113.

[34]Dietzgen, "The Nature of Human Brain–Work," in *Positive Outcome*, 71–180; Dietzgen, "The Excursion of a Socialist into the Domain of Epistemology," in *Some of the Philosophical Essays*, 263–362.

[35]Gorter, *Der historische Materialismus*, 113: "*Wo Marx aufzeigte, was die gesellschaftliche Materie an dem Geiste tut, zeigt Dietzgen was der Geist selbst tut.*"

[36]Dietzgen, *Positive Outcome*, 71.

[37]*Ibid.*, 87. Pannekoek has somewhat condensed Dietzgen's text.

[38]*Ibid.*, 119.

[39]*Ibid.*, 101–102.

[40]The German text reads: "*Den Gang der Lichtstrahlen kann man, anstatt durch dieses Gesetz, ebensogut durch das Prinzep des »kürzesten Lichtweges« wiedergeben.*" Pannekoek's decision to introduce an anthropomorphic description into his English translation is unfortunate, especially given his scientific training. Indeed, the present work does not suggest Pannekoek had as yet thoroughly digested the significance of Einsteinian physics for his own rather antiquated (and heavily

influenced by the layman Dietzgen) philosophy of science. In any case, Snell's 'least time principle' for the path of light cannot be reduced to a simple 'shorthand account' of the laws of classical geometrical (terrestrial scale) optics; rather, its full explanation demands an interpretation of light as a wave (which Pannekoek mocks) and, on an astronomical scale, the invocation of relativistic space–time. See Richard P. Feynman, *Feynman Lectures on Physics*, 3 vols., eds. Robert B. Leighton and Matthew Sands (Boston: Addison–Wesley, 1970), Chap. 26.

[41]The English freethinker Karl Pearson (1857–1936), whom Lenin mentions several times in *Materialism and Empirio–criticism*, was a gifted mathematician whose *The Grammar of Science* (London: Walter Scott, 1892) constitutes both a major advance in the scientific methods of mathematical analysis and an important forerunner of the theory of relativity. Like Haeckel, he later developed an interest in the application of statistical analysis to human biological characteristics in an effort to demonstrate the natural superiority of European races. Pearson spent the last 25 years of his life as Professor of Eugenics at the University College London. Gustav Kirchhoff (1824–1887), German physicist, taught at the University of Heidelberg from 1857 onwards. His work on black–body radiation played an important role in the later development of both Maxwell's electromagnetic theory and quantum mechanics. Jules Henri Poincaré (1854–1912), the great French mathematician and scientist, founded the science of qualitative dynamics and laid much of the foundations for Chaos theory in mathematics. In addition, he was a major figure in the philosophy of science, arguing against both Kant and Newton for a conventionalist description of spatial geometry, which debate became quite heated following Einstein's work in the early twentieth century. All three men were important figures in the conceptual revolution which natural science underwent in the later years of the nineteenth century as Classical Mechanics and the Newtonian worldview came unraveled. Pannekoek's derision of them as mystics and idealists is unhelpful, at best.

[42]Poincaré is ultimately a more important theorist than Mach, and his influence in the twentieth century has almost certainly been greater. See *Science and Convention: Essays on Henri Poincaré's Philosophy of Science and the Conventionalist Tradition*, J. Giedymin, ed. (Oxford: Oxford University Press, 1982) for a more recent appreciation of his significance for modern science.

[43]Ernst Mach, *The Analysis of Sensations and the Relation of the Physical to the Psychical*, trans. C. M. Williams and Sydney Waterlow; introduction by Thomas S. Szasz (New York: Dover, 1959), 29.

[44]*Ibid.*, 23–24.

[45]Ernst Mach, *The Science of Mechanics: A Critical and Historical Account of Its Development*, 6th ed. with revisions through the 9th German edition, trans. Thomas J. McCormack; new introduction by Karl Menger (La Salle, IL: Open Court, 1960), 579.

[46]*Ibid.*, 577, 578–79.

[47]Mach, *The Analysis of Sensations*, 37.

[48]Mach, *The Science of Mechanics*, 586.

[49]Mach, *The Analysis of Sensations*, 35.

[50]Mach, *The Science of Mechanics*, 559.

[51]Mach, *The Analysis of Sensations*, 12.

[52]*Ibid.*, 361.

[53] *Ibid.*, 44, 17–18.

[54] Ernst Mach, *Knowledge and Error: Sketches on the Psychology of Inquiry*, trans. Thomas J. McCormack and Paul Foulkes (Boston: D. Reidle, 1976), 12.

[55] Rudolf Carnap, *The Logical Structure of the World: Pseudoproblems in Philosophy*, trans. Rolf A. George (Berkeley: University of California Press, 1967). It should be noted that the Vienna Circle from which Logical Positivism arose was originally formed by Moritz Schlick under the name *Ernst Mach Verein* (Ernst Mach Association). For further discussion of Carnap's relationship to Mach, see Carnap's own acknowledgement of influence in *Wissenschaftliche Weltauffassung: Der Wiener Kreis*, herausgegeben vom Verein Ernst Mach, preface signed by Hans Hahn, Rudolf Carnap and Otto Neurath (Wien: Artur Wolf, 1929); Arnold Keyserling, *Der Weiner Denkstil: Mach, Carnap, Wittgenstein* (Graz und Vien: Stiashy Verlag, 1981).

[56] Mach, *The Analysis of Sensations*, 12.

[57] *Ibid.*, 37.

[58] Mach, *The Science of Mechanics*, 588–89, 599.

[59] Richard Avenarius, *Kritik der reinen Erfahrung*, 3. Aufl., 2 vols. (Leipzig: Reisland, 1928). Pannekoek's reference to this work is not particularly relevant since all his quotations are from Avenarius' *Die Menschliche Weltbegriff* (Leipzig: O. R. Reisland, 1927). The German text of Pannekoek (Europäische Verlagsanst Frankfurt, 1969) and both English editions (New York: New Essays, 1948; London: Merlin, 1975) leave this mistake uncorrected. None of Avenarius' works have been translated into English.

[60] Avenarius, *Die Menschliche Weltbegriff*, 9.

[61] *Ibid.*, 57.

[62] *Ibid.*, 68.

[63] *Ibid.*, 76.

[64] *Ibid.*, 234–235.

[65] *Ibid.*, 200–201.

[66] *CW* 14:42.

[67] *CW* 14:42. Joseph Petzoldt (1862–1929) was an Austrian empirio–critical philosopher and supporter of the views of Avernarius. His chief work was *Das Weltproblem vom Standpunkte des relativistischen Positivismus aus historisch–kristisch dargestellt* (Leipzig und Berlin: D. G. Teubner, 1906).

[68] *CW* 14:43.

[69] *CW* 14:150–51.

[70] *CW* 14:54.

[71] Reference unclear, probably to Mach, *The Analysis of Sensations*, 61. If so, Pannekoek is quoting Mach quite loosely.

[72] *CW* 14:54.

[73] Avenarius, *Die Menschliche Weltbegriff*, 190.

[74] *CW* 14:57.

[75] *CW* 14:87.

[76] *CW* 14:88–89.

[77] *CW* 14:72–73. Norman Kemp Smith (1872–1958), most famous for his translations of and commentaries on Kant, contributed several articles to the debate over Machism and empirio–criticism during the first decade of the twentieth century. Wilhelm Schuppe (1836–1913), German philosopher, was co–editor of *Zeitschrift*

für immanente Philosophie. Immanentism was a radically empiricist movement in late nineteenth century German philosophy which provided an important backdrop for the work of the Vienna Circle. Peter Struve (1870–1944), Russian Marxist and leader of the Constitutional Democratic Party (Cadets) which opposed the Bolshevik seizure of power, emigrated to France after their suppression by the Bolsheviks following the October Revolution. M. O. Menshikov (1859–1919) was a reactionary journalist and editor of *Novoye Vremya*, a St. Petersburg daily of militantly tasrist bent eventually suppressed by the Bolsheviks.

[78] *Wilhelm Schuppe, "Offener Briefe an Avernarius über die 'Bestätigung des Naiven Realismus,"* in Avenarius, *Die Meschlische Weltbegriff,* 135–178.

[79] *CW* 14:51.

[80] *CW* 14:46.

[81] *CW* 14:146.

[82] *CW* 14:161.

[83] *CW* 14:159.

[84] *CW* 14:160.

[85] *CW* 14:160.

[86] *CW* 14:160.

[87] *CW* 14:170.

[88] *CW* 14:170.

[89] Gustav Kirchhoff, *Vorlesungen über Mathematische Physik* (Leipzig: B.G. Teubner, 1877), 1.

[90] *CW* 14:171.

[91] *CW* 14:177–78.

[92] Mach, *The Science of Mechanics*, 592.

[93] *CW 14:181.*

[94] Mach, *The Science of Mechanics*, 611.

[95] *CW* 14:179.

[96] *CW* 14:181.

[97] *CW* 14:130.

[98] Wilhelm Ostwald, *Natural Philosophy,* tr. Thomas Seltzer (New York: Henry Holt & Co., 1910), 138. Ostwald (1853–1932), a leading German chemist and(1853–1932), a leading German chemist and professor at Leipzig, won the Noble Prize in Chemistry in 1909.

[99] Dietzgen, *Positive Outcome*, 204. Pannekoek condenses and quotes very loosely here.

[100] *CW* 14:243–44.

[101] *CW* 14:92.

[102] *CW* 14:47.

[103] Frederick Engels, *Anti–Dühring, MECW* 25:71.

[104] Georgi Plekhanov, *Fundamental Problems of Marxism,* in *Selected Philosophical Works,* 5 vols., 3rd ed. (Moscow: Progress Publishers, 1977), 3:117–183, 141. All Plekhanov references are to this edition; the method of citation follows that for Lenin and Marx. Pannekoek quotes loosely here.

[105] *CW* 14:240–41.

[106] *CW* 14:242.

[107] *CW* 14:256.

[108] *CW* 14:191.

[109]*CW* 14:348.

[110]*CW* 14:350. Pannekoek quotes Lenin somewhat loosely here.

[111]*CW* 14:350, 352. Pannekoek quotes Lenin quite loosely here.

[112]*CW* 14:348–49.

[113]Ernest Haeckel, *Freedom in Science and Teaching*, tr. T. H. Huxley (New York: D. Appleton and Co., 1879), 92.

[114]Plekhanov, *Selected Philosophical Works*, 3:124.

[115]*Ibid.*, 3:124–125.

[116]*Ibid.*, 3:128.

[117]*Ibid.*, 3:129.

[118]Mikhail Ivanovich Tugan–Baranovsky (1865–1919), Russian economist, pioneered modern research into business cycles. His work was followed by some Marxists who disavowed Marx's belief in the inevitability of economic crises within capitalism.

[119]Plekhanov, *Essays in the History of Materialism*, in *Selected Philosophical Works*, 2:31–182.

[120]*CW* 34:379–82, 381. Pannekoek quotes Lenin loosely here but accurately conveys his attitude towards Bogdanov, Lunacharsky, and other empirio–critics. No specific title he may have read is mentioned in the letter.

[121]*CW* 14:358.

Name Index

Subject Index